THIS BOOK GIVEN TO

_____

GIVEN BY

_____

DATE

_____

ISBN 978-1-60587-522-4
ISBN 978-1-60587-544-6 (special edition)

Published by Freeman-Smith, a division of Worthy Media, Inc.,
134 Franklin Road, Suite 200, Brentwood, Tennessee 37027.

The quoted ideas expressed in this book (but not Scripture verses) are not, in all cases, exact quotations, as some have been edited for clarity and brevity. In all cases, the author has attempted to maintain the speaker's original intent. In some cases, quoted material for this book was obtained from secondary sources, primarily print media. While every effort was made to ensure the accuracy of these sources, the accuracy cannot be guaranteed. For additions, deletions, corrections, or clarifications in future editions of this text, please write Freeman-Smith.

"Redeemed" © 2012 Weave Country (Admin. by Word Music, LLC), Word Music, LLC. Benji Cowart/ Michael Weaver. All Rights Reserved. Used By Permission.

Scripture quotations are taken from:

The Holy Bible, King James Version (KJV)

The Holy Bible, New International Version (NIV) Copyright © 1973, 1978, 1984, by International Bible Society. Used by permission of Zondervan Publishing House. All rights reserved.

The Holy Bible, New King James Version (NKJV) Copyright © 1982 by Thomas Nelson, Inc. Used by permission.

Holy Bible, New Living Translation, (NLT) copyright © 1996. Used by permission of Tyndale House Publishers, Inc., Wheaton, Illinois 60189. All rights reserved.

The Message (MSG)- This edition issued by contractual arrangement with NavPress, a division of The Navigators, U.S.A. Originally published by NavPress in English as THE MESSAGE: The Bible in Contemporary Language copyright 2002-2003 by Eugene Peterson. All rights reserved.

New Century Version®. (NCV) Copyright © 1987, 1988, 1991 by Word Publishing, a division of Thomas Nelson, Inc. All rights reserved. Used by permission.

The ESV® Bible (The Holy Bible, English Standard Version®) copyright © 2001 by Crossway, a publishing ministry of Good News Publishers. ESV® Text Edition: 2011. The ESV® text has been reproduced in cooperation with and by permission of Good News Publishers. Unauthorized reproduction of this publication is prohibited. All rights reserved.

The New American Standard Bible®, (NASB) Copyright © 1960, 1962, 1963, 1968, 1971, 1972, 1973, 1975, 1977, 1995 by The Lockman Foundation. Used by permission.

The Holman Christian Standard Bible™ (HCSB) Copyright © 1999, 2000, 2001 by Holman Bible Publishers. Used by permission.

Cover Design by Greg Jackson / ThinkpenDesign.com
Page Layout by Bart Dawson

Printed in the United States of America

1 2 3 4 5—SBI—17 16 15 14 13

REDEEMED

A Devotional Based on the #1 Song

That Has Inspired Millions

FREEMAN-SMITH

TABLE OF CONTENTS

Let the words of my mouth
and the meditation of my heart
be acceptable in Your sight, O Lord,
my strength and my Redeemer.

—

Psalm 19:14 NKJV

DEDICATED TO:

To all of our friends and family
who have been a part of what
God is doing through
this special song.

REDEEMED

by Mike Weaver of Big Daddy Weave and Benji Cowart

Seems like all I can see was the struggle
Haunted by ghosts that lived in my past
Bound up in shackles of all my failures
Wondering how long is this gonna last
Then You look at this prisoner and say to me
"son stop fighting a fight that's already been won"

I am redeemed, You set me free
So I'll shake off these heavy chains
Wipe away every stain now I'm not who I used to be
I am redeemed

All my life I have been called unworthy
Named by the voice of my shame and regret
But when I hear You whisper, "Child lift up your head"
I remember oh God, You're not done with me yet

I don't have to be the old man inside of me
Cause his day is long dead and gone
I've got a new name, a new life I'm not the same
And a hope that will carry me home

A MESSAGE TO READERS

FROM MIKE WEAVER OF BIG DADDY WEAVE

The song "Redeemed" comes from a difficult time in my life. I was really at a low point, struggling with my imperfections, when I felt like God said to my spirit, "Why don't you let me tell you what I think about you and what I like about you?" He started with, "I love your heart for people," and went from there. I was like a broken heap on the floor of my garage. The things He was talking about were not future tense things. Like a lot of people, I think, "If I could get to this point and look like this and achieve that, I would be all right." But He has this "I love who you are right now" mentality—"I accept you right now. You need to accept you right now."

When my friend, Benji Cowart, and I got together on Skype and wrote "Redeemed," we never imagined the impact it would have. I had no idea, even after we finished it, that God would do what He's done with this song. In my mind, it was just some closure to a really rough season in my walk with Jesus. Only God can take what we're most ashamed of and turn it into victory! I'm so thankful for the way He's used this song in the lives of so many. And, I continue to thank Him daily that the words of this song are true in my life.

The thirty devotionals in this book are reminders that God sent His Son so that we all might experience the life-changing power of redemption. During the next month, read a chapter each day. When you do, I wouldn't be surprised if you find yourself hearing God speak to your heart as He did to mine, to see yourself as He sees you—Redeemed.

CHAPTER 1

REDEEMED FROM THE GHOSTS OF THE PAST

The one who acquires good sense loves himself; one who safeguards understanding finds success.

—

Proverbs 19:8 HCSB

All of us have regrets—ghosts from the past that we'd rather ignore or forget. But, no matter how hard we try, we cannot change the past, and we cannot redeem ourselves. Only God can do that, and He is willing, ready, and able.

Do you invest more time than you should reliving the past? Are you troubled by feelings of anger, bitterness, envy, or regret? Do you harbor ill will against someone you can't seem to forgive?

Perhaps there's something in your past that you deeply regret. Or maybe you've been scarred by a trauma that you simply can't seem to resolve. If so, it's time to ask for God's help—sincerely and prayerfully. You can choose to give it to Him, once and for all, to move beyond yesterday's pain and walk in the fullness of what God has purchased for you in Christ Jesus.

It's natural to fret over the injustices you've suffered and to hold grudges against the people who inflicted them. But God has a better plan: He wants you to supernaturally live in the present, not the past. By the power of the Holy Spirit, you can forgive and, by doing so, move on.

MORE PROMISES FROM GOD'S WORD

Do not remember the past events, pay no attention to things of old. Look, I am about to do something new; even now it is coming. Do you not see it? Indeed, I will make a way in the wilderness, rivers in the desert.

Isaiah 43:18-19 HCSB

I do not consider myself yet to have taken hold of it. But one thing I do: Forgetting what is behind and straining toward what is ahead, I press on toward the goal to win the prize for which God has called me heavenward in Christ Jesus.

Philippians 3:13-14 NIV

And He who sits on the throne said, "Behold, I am making all things new."

Revelation 21:5 NASB

Your old life is dead. Your new life, which is your real life—even though invisible to spectators—is with Christ in God. He is your life.

Colossians 3:3 MSG

MORE GREAT IDEAS

If you are God's child, you are no longer bound to your past or to what you were. You are a brand new creature in Christ Jesus.

Kay Arthur

We set our eyes on the finish line, forgetting the past, and straining toward the mark of spiritual maturity and fruitfulness.

Vonette Bright

The devil keeps so many of us stuck in our weakness. He reminds us of our pasts when we ought to remind him of his future—he doesn't have one.

Franklin Graham

We need to be at peace with our past, content with our present, and sure about our future, knowing they are all in God's hands.

Joyce Meyer

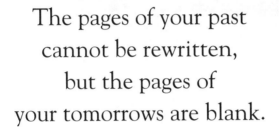

The pages of your past
cannot be rewritten,
but the pages of
your tomorrows are blank.

—

Zig Ziglar

A TIMELY TIP

The past is past, so don't invest all your energy there. If you're focused on the past, change your focus. If you're living in the past, move on.

A PRAYER FOR TODAY

Heavenly Father, free me from anger, resentment, and envy. When I am bitter, I cannot feel the peace that You intend for my life. Keep me mindful that forgiveness is Your commandment, and help me accept the past, treasure the present, and trust the future to You. Amen

YOUR OWN THOUGHTS ABOUT
ACCEPTING THE PAST AND MOVING ON

CHAPTER 2

REDEEMED
FROM THE TEARS

I have heard your prayer;
I have seen your tears.
Look, I will heal you.

—

2 Kings 20:5 HCSB

In periods of grief, the enemy's efforts can cause you to wonder if you'll ever recover. When the feelings of sorrow are most intense, his lie is that the pain will never subside. But the good news is this: while time heals many wounds, God has the power to heal them all, for His truth triumphs over any lie of the enemy.

Ours is a God of infinite power, infinite mercy, and infinite possibilities. Ask Him for His help to walk in the healing purchased for you by Jesus' blood. Thank Him for leading you into His peace that passes all understanding. Abandon your doubts and confess God's promises.

> A teardrop on earth summons the King of Heaven.
>
> —
>
> *Charles Swindoll*

God's Word makes it clear: absolutely nothing is impossible for Him. Be comforted in the knowledge that the Creator of the universe can do miraculous things in your life and in the lives of your loved ones. Take God at His word and wait expectantly on Him, knowing that He is faithful to do what He says He will do.

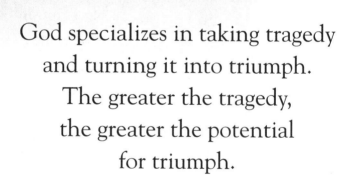

God specializes in taking tragedy
and turning it into triumph.
The greater the tragedy,
the greater the potential
for triumph.

—

Charles Stanley

MORE PROMISES FROM GOD'S WORD

I called to the Lord in my distress; I called to my God. From His temple He heard my voice.

2 Samuel 22:7 HCSB

Blessed are you who are hungry now, because you will be filled. Blessed are you who weep now, because you will laugh.

Luke 6:21 HCSB

Blessed are the poor in spirit, for theirs is the kingdom of heaven. Blessed are those who mourn, for they shall be comforted.

Matthew 5:3-4 NKJV

Lord, how long will You continually forget me? How long will You hide Your face from me?

Psalm 13:1 HCSB

When I sit in darkness, the Lord will be a light to me.

Micah 7:8 NKJV

MORE GREAT IDEAS

Our valleys may be filled with foes and tears, but we can lift our eyes to the hills to see God and the angels.

Billy Graham

The joy of God is experienced as I love, trust, and obey God—no matter the circumstances—and as I allow Him to do in and through me whatever He wishes, thanking Him that in every pain there is pleasure, in every suffering there is satisfaction, in every aching there is comfort, in every sense of loss there is the surety of the Savior's presence, and in every tear there is the glistening eye of God.

Bill Bright

The God of the galaxies is the God who knows when your heart is broken—and He can heal it!

Warren Wiersbe

The grace of God is sufficient for all our needs, for every problem and for every difficulty, for every broken heart, and for every human sorrow.

Peter Marshall

A TIMELY TIP

Grief is a part of our lives, as are God's promises to heal our hearts. Seek Him and rest in His love.

A PRAYER FOR TODAY

Lord, thank You for being there for me in my grief. Thank You for Your strength today, tomorrow, and forever. Amen

YOUR OWN THOUGHTS ABOUT GRIEF AND HEALING

CHAPTER 3

REDEEMED FROM REGRET

Do not remember the past events,
pay no attention to things of old. Look,
I am about to do something new;
even now it is coming. Do you not see it?
Indeed, I will make a way in
the wilderness, rivers in the desert.

—

Isaiah 43:18-19 HCSB

We've all heard the saying "Don't cry over spilt milk." While that sounds simple, we know sometimes that's easier said than done. Maybe you deal with regret over times in your life you have failed. Maybe there's regret over things that have happened to you, or over opportunities missed. While we could choose to live in regret, we don't have to dwell on the disappointments and failures. When we trust God's Word, follow Jesus, and accept His redemption, we find hope in His plans for the future (Jer. 29:11).

> Sold for thirty pieces of silver, he redeemed the world.
>
> —
>
> *R. G. Lee*

Living in regret over a past defeat can become spiritual sickness, an emotionally destructive mindset that can rob you of happiness and peace.

Ask the Holy Spirit to reveal to you whenever feelings of anger or bitterness are invading your thoughts. Recognize and resist negative thoughts before they hijack your emotions by letting God rescue you from your regrets.

MORE PROMISES FROM GOD'S WORD

One thing I do, forgetting those things which are behind and reaching forward to those things which are ahead, I press toward the goal for the prize of the upward call of God in Christ Jesus.

Philippians 3:13-14 NKJV

Consider it a great joy, my brothers, whenever you experience various trials, knowing that the testing of your faith produces endurance. But endurance must do its complete work, so that you may be mature and complete, lacking nothing.

James 1:2-4 HCSB

Be strong and courageous, and do the work. Do not be afraid or discouraged, for the Lord God, my God, is with you.

1 Chronicles 28:20 NIV

The Lord is my light and my salvation; whom shall I fear? The Lord is the strength of my life; of whom shall I be afraid?

Psalm 27:1 KJV

MORE GREAT IDEAS

Get rid of the poison of built-up anger and the acid of long-term resentment.

Charles Swindoll

In the Christian story God descends to reascend. He comes down; . . . down to the very roots and sea-bed of the Nature he has created. But He goes down to come up again and bring the whole ruined world with Him.

C. S. Lewis

The enemy of our souls loves to taunt us with past failures, wrongs, disappointments, disasters, and calamities. And if we let him continue doing this, our life becomes a long and dark tunnel, with very little light at the end.

Charles Swindoll

He is ever faithful and gives us the song in the night to soothe our spirits and fresh joy each morning to lift our souls. What a marvelous Lord!

Bill Bright

Like a spring of pure water,
God's peace in our hearts
brings cleansing and refreshment
to our minds and bodies.

—

Billy Graham

> Make the least of all that goes and the most of all that comes. Don't regret what is past. Cherish what you have. Look forward to all that is to come. And most important of all, rely moment by moment on Jesus Christ.
>
> —
>
> *Gigi Graham Tchividjian*

A PRAYER FOR TODAY

Heavenly Father, free me from regret, resentment, and anger. When I am bitter, I cannot feel the peace that You intend for my life. Keep me mindful that forgiveness is Your commandment, and help me accept the past, treasure the present, and trust the future to You. Amen

YOUR OWN THOUGHTS ABOUT MOVING PAST REGRET

CHAPTER 4

REDEEMED FROM THE SHAME

Be gracious to me, God, according to Your faithful love; according to Your abundant compassion, blot out my rebellion. Wash away my guilt, and cleanse me from my sin.

—

Psalm 51:1-2 HCSB

Have you done things you're ashamed of? If so, welcome to a very large club . . . all of us! Everyone on the planet is a member. But the good news is this: Whenever we admit our shortcomings to God and ask for His forgiveness, He gives it.

There's nothing any of us can do to redeem ourselves from sin; that's something only God can do. So what can we do? We can allow Jesus into our hearts and allow Him to do what we cannot.

Shame is a form of spiritual cancer; it is deadly, but it is treatable. The treatment begins when we acknowledge our sins and ask for God's mercy. But, it doesn't end there. Once God forgives us, we need to see ourselves the way He sees us . . . innocent.

God knows all your imperfections, all your faults, and all your shortcomings. He paid for every one of them with the blood of Jesus. He loves you unconditionally. There is nothing you can do to make Him love you more or less. And because God loves you, you can feel good about the person you see when you look into the mirror. God's love is bigger and more powerful than any of us can imagine. Accept it with open arms. Remember today that even when you don't love yourself very much, God loves you. And you need to love what He loves, because God is always right.

MORE PROMISES FROM GOD'S WORD

I waited patiently for the LORD; he turned to me and heard my cry. He lifted me out of the slimy pit, out of the mud and mire; he set my feet on a rock and gave me a firm place to stand. He put a new song in my mouth, a hymn of praise to our God....

Psalm 40:1-3 NIV

Therefore, if anyone is in Christ, he is a new creation; the old has gone, the new has come!

2 Corinthians 5:17 NIV

Have mercy on me, O God, according to your unfailing love; according to your great compassion blot out my transgressions. Wash away all my iniquity and cleanse me from my sin.

Psalm 51:1-2 NIV

MORE GREAT IDEAS

One of Satan's most effective ploys is to make us believe that we are small, insignificant, and worthless.

Susan Lenzkes

The soul that still is in some way hiding cannot enjoy the fullness of knowing what characterizes the love between God and the saints in heaven.

John Eldredge

You are valuable just because you exist. Not because of what you do or what you have done, but simply because you are.

Max Lucado

You are valuable because God values you.

Stanley Grenz

How changed our lives would be if we could only fly through the days on wings of surrender and trust!

Hannah Whitall Smith

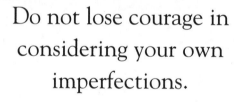

Do not lose courage in
considering your own
imperfections.

—

St. Francis de Sales

Christianity is about acceptance,
and if God accepts me as I am,
then I had better do the same.

—

Hugh Montefiore

A PRAYER FOR TODAY

Dear Lord, I am an imperfect human being. When I have sinned, let me repent from my wrongdoings and not live in shame. Let me seek forgiveness—first from You, then from others, and finally from myself. Amen

YOUR OWN THOUGHTS ABOUT
FREEING YOURSELF FROM SHAME

CHAPTER 5

REDEEMED FROM FAILURE

*If we confess our sins to him,
he is faithful and just to forgive us
and to cleanse us from every wrong.*

—

1 John 1:9 NLT

The occasional disappointments and failures of life are inevitable, but we must never lose faith even when we encounter what we may perceive as bitter setbacks.

The reassuring words of Hebrews 10:36 have this advice: "Patient endurance is what you need now, so you will continue to do God's will. Then you will receive all that He has promised." These words serve as a reminder that while we persevere, we can look forward to receiving that which God has promised. Perseverance is the continued walk in faith, the pursuing each day our relationship with God and the actions to which He calls us.

> If you learn from a defeat, you have not really lost.
>
> —
>
> *Zig Ziglar*

His plan is perfect. Step forward in that knowledge, over and through past failures, walking in confidence and expectation of His mercies and blessings.

MORE PROMISES FROM GOD'S WORD

If you hide your sins, you will not succeed. If you confess and reject them, you will receive mercy.

Proverbs 28:13 NCV

If you listen to constructive criticism, you will be at home among the wise.

Proverbs 15:31 NLT

So we're not giving up. How could we! Even though on the outside it often looks like things are falling apart on us, on the inside, where God is making new life, not a day goes by without his unfolding grace.

2 Corinthians 4:16 MSG

I waited patiently for the LORD; he turned to me and heard my cry. He lifted me out of the slimy pit, out of the mud and mire; he set my feet on a rock and gave me a firm place to stand. He put a new song in my mouth, a hymn of praise to our God....

Psalm 40:1-3 NIV

MORE GREAT IDEAS

No matter how badly we have failed, we can always get up and begin again. Our God is the God of new beginnings.

Warren Wiersbe

Mistakes offer the possibility for redemption and a new start in God's kingdom. No matter what you're guilty of, God can restore your innocence.

Barbara Johnson

Lord, when we are wrong, make us willing to change; and when we are right, make us easy to live with.

Peter Marshall

The enemy of our souls loves to taunt us with past failures, wrongs, disappointments, disasters, and calamities. And if we let him continue doing this, our life becomes a long and dark tunnel, with very little light at the end.

Charles Swindoll

It is true of every stinging
experience of our lives:
Jesus, and Jesus alone,
can rescue us.

—

Franklin Graham

A TIMELY TIP

Setbacks are inevitable. Your response to them is optional.

A PRAYER FOR TODAY

Dear Lord, when I encounter failures and disappointments, keep me mindful that You are in control. Let me persevere and follow Your Son, Jesus Christ, this day and forever. Amen

YOUR OWN THOUGHTS ABOUT
MOVING PAST FAILURE

CHAPTER 6

REDEEMED TO PLEASE HIM FIRST

*For am I now trying to win
the favor of people, or God?
Or am I striving to please people?
If I were still trying to please people,
I would not be a slave of Christ.*

—

Galatians 1:10 HCSB

Peer pressure is everywhere. You may, from time to time, feel the urge by those around you to act or be a certain way.

Peer pressure can be good or bad, depending upon who your peers are and how they behave. If your friends encourage you to follow God's will and to obey His commandments, then you'll experience positive peer pressure, and that's a good thing. But, if your friends encourage you to do things counter to what you know are God's desires, then you're facing a different kind of peer pressure . . . don't give in! When you feel pressured to do or say things that lead you away from God, you're heading straight for trouble. So don't do the "easy" thing or the "popular" thing. Do the right thing, and don't worry about winning any popularity contests. The choices you make in those moments will not only impact your life, but can also impact the lives of others who are watching.

God can redeem you from the dangers of negative peer pressure and use your life to be a light to those around you. You rise above the world's pressures when you decide to follow Jesus. When you accept His redemption, God will guide your steps and bless your undertakings.

MORE PROMISES FROM GOD'S WORD

He who walks with wise men will be wise, but the companion of fools will be destroyed.

Proverbs 13:20 NKJV

Stay away from a foolish man; you will gain no knowledge from his speech.

Proverbs 14:7 HCSB

My son, if sinners entice you, don't be persuaded.

Proverbs 1:10 HCSB

Blessed is the man who walks not in the counsel of the ungodly, nor stands in the path of sinners, nor sits in the seat of the scornful; but his delight is in the law of the Lord, and in His law he meditates day and night.

Psalm 1:1-2 NKJV

Do not be deceived: "Bad company corrupts good morals."

1 Corinthians 15:33 HCSB

MORE GREAT IDEAS

Those who follow the crowd usually get lost in it.

Rick Warren

Comparison is the root of all feelings of inferiority.

James Dobson

It is impossible to please God doing things motivated by and produced by the flesh.

Bill Bright

It is comfortable to know that we are responsible to God and not to man. It is a small matter to be judged of man's judgement.

Lottie Moon

People who constantly, and fervently, seek the approval of others live with an identity crisis. They don't know who they are, and they are defined by what others think of them.

Charles Stanley

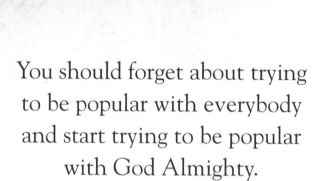

You should forget about trying
to be popular with everybody
and start trying to be popular
with God Almighty.

—

Sam Jones

A TIMELY TIP

Seek to please God first in all you do. Then, choosing from all the other influences will be easier to discern.

A PRAYER FOR TODAY

Dear Lord, today I will worry less about pleasing other people and more about pleasing You. I will honor You with my thoughts, my actions, and my prayers. And I will worship You, Father, with thanksgiving in my heart. Amen

YOUR OWN THOUGHTS ABOUT
PEER PRESSURE AND ITS CONSEQUENCES

CHAPTER 7

REDEEMED FROM THE STRUGGLE

I called to the Lord in my distress;
I called to my God.
From His temple He heard my voice.

—

2 Samuel 22:7 HCSB

Perhaps you've heard the saying, "When you get to the end of your rope, tie a knot and hold on for dear life." Seems like sound advice, but here's something else to think about: As a believer, when you get to the end of your rope, you are never alone because God is right there with you. You don't have to try to hold on with your own strength because God's strength is the ultimate power and the ultimate protection.

> The hope we have in Jesus is the anchor for the soul—something sure and steadfast, preventing drifting or giving way, lowered to the depth of God's love.
>
> —
>
> *Franklin Graham*

No matter where you are, no matter how desperate your circumstances, God never leaves you, not even for an instant. You belong to Him—you are His precious child and His one-of-a-kind creation.

So the next time you find yourself at the end of your rope, don't worry. God is bigger than anything you could ever face and He is for you!

MORE PROMISES FROM GOD'S WORD

We also have joy with our troubles, because we know that these troubles produce patience. And patience produces character, and character produces hope.

Romans 5:3-4 NCV

The LORD also will be a stronghold for the oppressed, a stronghold in times of trouble.

Psalm 9:9 NASB

Come to Me, all you who labor and are heavy laden, and I will give you rest. Take My yoke upon you and learn from Me, for I am gentle and lowly in heart, and you will find rest for your souls. For My yoke is easy and My burden is light.

Matthew 11:28-30 NKJV

Consider it a great joy, my brothers, whenever you experience various trials, knowing that the testing of your faith produces endurance. But endurance must do its complete work, so that you may be mature and complete, lacking nothing.

James 1:2-4 HCSB

MORE GREAT IDEAS

Any man can sing in the day. It is easy to sing when we can read the notes by daylight, but he is the skillful singer who can sing when there is not a ray of light by which to read. Songs in the night come only from God; they are not in the power of man.

C. H. Spurgeon

If your every human plan and calculation has miscarried, if, one by one, human props have been knocked out...take heart. God is trying to get a message through to you, and the message is: "Stop depending on inadequate human resources. Let me handle the matter."

Catherine Marshall

Oh, remember this: There is never a time when we may not hope in God. Whatever our necessities, however great our difficulties, and though to all appearance, help is impossible, yet our business is to hope in God, and it will be found that it is not in vain.

George Mueller

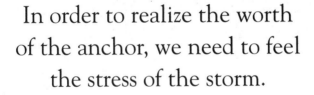

In order to realize the worth
of the anchor, we need to feel
the stress of the storm.

—

Corrie ten Boom

A TIMELY TIP

If you're having tough times, don't go through them alone. Talk things over with people you can really trust. Be willing to seek help from family members, trusted friends, and your pastor.

A PRAYER FOR TODAY

Lord, sometimes life is tough . . . very tough. But even when I can't see any hope for the future, I know You are always with me. I can live courageously because I know that You are almighty, my rock and my strength. Amen

YOUR OWN THOUGHTS ABOUT
THE STRUGGLES YOU FACE

CHAPTER 8

REDEEMED
BY HIS PROMISES

*Let us hold on to the confession
of our hope without wavering,
for He who promised is faithful.*

—

Hebrews 10:23 HCSB

God has made many promises to you, and He will keep every single one of them. He has promised to redeem you from your sins. In fact, He's already done it. He did it many years ago on a distant hill at Calvary.

You can trust God's Word in every situation you will ever encounter. No exceptions.

Are you facing a difficult decision? Pause for a moment and have a quiet consultation with your ultimate Advisor. Are you fearful, anxious, fretful, or troubled? Slow yourself down long enough to consider God's promises. Are you going through a difficult period of your life? Ask God to help you, after all that's precisely what He's promised to do.

God's promises never fail and they never grow old. Rely upon those promises, share them with your family, with your friends, and with the world.

> We can have full confidence in God's promises because we can have full faith in His character.
>
> —
>
> *Franklin Graham*

MORE PROMISES FROM GOD'S WORD

Trust in the Lord with all your heart, and do not rely on your own understanding; think about Him in all your ways, and He will guide you on the right paths.

Proverbs 3:5-6 HCSB

God also bound himself with an oath, so that those who received the promise could be perfectly sure that he would never change his mind. So God has given us both his promise and his oath. These two things are unchangeable because it is impossible for God to lie. Therefore, we who have fled to him for refuge can take new courage, for we can hold on to his promise with confidence.

Hebrews 6:17-18 NLT

Whatever God has promised gets stamped with the Yes of Jesus. In him, this is what we preach and pray, the great Amen, God's Yes and our Yes together, gloriously evident.

2 Corinthians 1:20 MSG

MORE GREAT IDEAS

We honor God by asking for great things when they are a part of His promise. We dishonor Him and cheat ourselves when we ask for molehills where He has promised mountains.

Vance Havner

God's promises are medicine for the broken heart. Let Him comfort you. And, after He has comforted you, try to share that comfort with somebody else. It will do both of you good.

Warren Wiersbe

Never doubt in the dark what God told you in the light.

V. Raymond Edman

The meaning of hope isn't just some flimsy wishing. It's a firm confidence in God's promises—that he will ultimately set things right.

Sheila Walsh

The stars may fall,
but God's promises will stand
and be fulfilled.

—

J. I. Packer

Claim all of God's promises in the Bible.
Your sins, your worries, your life—
you may cast them all on Him.

—

Corrie ten Boom

A PRAYER FOR TODAY

Lord, Your Holy Word contains promises, and I will trust them. I will use the Bible as my guide, and I will trust You, Lord, to speak to me through Your Holy Spirit and through Your Holy Word, this day and forever. Amen

YOUR OWN THOUGHTS ABOUT A DIFFICULT
DECISION YOU NEED TO PRAY ABOUT

CHAPTER 9

REDEEMED AND BRAND NEW

If anyone belongs to Christ,
there is a new creation.
The old things have gone;
everything is made new!

—

2 Corinthians 5:17 NCV

Giving your heart to Christ means that you're willing to take a risk. After all, when you commit your mind, body, and soul to God, you know that you'll be giving up many of the things that the world holds dear. But with that risk come unimaginable rewards: the gift of eternal life, the peace that passes all understanding, and the knowledge that you've been redeemed by the incredible sacrifice of God's Son.

Inviting God's Son to reign over your heart invites Him to take over and make over every part of your life. Warren Wiersbe observed, "The greatest miracle of all is the transformation of a lost sinner into a child of God." And Oswald Chambers noted, "If the Spirit of God has transformed you within, you will exhibit Divine characteristics in your life, not good human characteristics. God's life in us expresses itself as God's life, not as a human life trying to be godly."

When you invited Christ to reign over your heart, you became a new creation through Him. This day offers yet another opportunity to walk in the new life given in Christ and thus strengthen the godly character within you. Let God guide your steps and bless your endeavors today and forever.

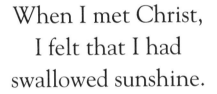

When I met Christ,
I felt that I had
swallowed sunshine.

—

E. Stanley Jones

MORE PROMISES FROM GOD'S WORD

Your old life is dead. Your new life, which is your real life—even though invisible to spectators—is with Christ in God. He is your life.

Colossians 3:3 MSG

You were taught to leave your old self—to stop living the evil way you lived before. That old self becomes worse, because people are fooled by the evil things they want to do. But you were taught to be made new in your hearts, to become a new person. That new person is made to be like God—made to be truly good and holy.

Ephesians 4:22–24 NCV

Jesus answered and said to him, "Truly, truly, I say to you, unless one is born again he cannot see the kingdom of God."

John 3:3 NASB

Therefore we were buried with Him by baptism into death, in order that, just as Christ was raised from the dead by the glory of the Father, so we too may walk in a new way of life.

Romans 6:4 HCSB

MORE GREAT IDEAS

God is not a supernatural interferer; God is the everlasting portion of his people. When a man born from above begins his new life, he meets God at every turn, hears him in every sound, sleeps at his feet, and wakes to find him there.

Oswald Chambers

Before God changes our circumstances, He wants to change our hearts.

Warren Wiersbe

No one can be converted except with the consent of his own free will because God does not override human choice.

Billy Graham

We had better quickly discover whether we have mere religion or a real experience with Jesus, whether we have outward observance of religious forms or hearts that beat in tune with God.

Jim Cymbala

> Salvation is not just a repairing
> of the original self.
> It is a new self created of God.
>
> —
>
> *Billy Graham*

A PRAYER FOR TODAY

Lord, when I accepted Jesus as my Savior, You redeemed me, changed me forever, and made me whole. Let me share Your Son's message with my friends, with my family, and with the world. You are a God of love, redemption, conversion, and salvation. I will praise You today and forever. Amen

YOUR OWN THOUGHTS ABOUT
TURNING EVERYTHING OVER TO JESUS

CHAPTER 10

REDEEMED BY A LOVING GOD

Jesus said to him, "'You shall love the Lord your God with all your heart, with all your soul, and with all your mind.' This is the first and great commandment."

—

Matthew 22:37-38 NKJV

Where can we find God's love? Everywhere. God's love transcends space and time. It reaches beyond the heavens, and it touches the darkest, smallest corner of every human heart. When we open our minds and hearts to God, His love does not arrive "someday"—it arrives immediately.

God loves our world so much that He sent His only begotten Son to redeem us. And now we, as believers, are challenged to return God's love by obeying His commandments and honoring His Son.

When you open your heart and accept God's love, you are transformed not just for today, but for all eternity. When you accept the Father's love, it affects the way you see and respond to yourself, your world, your neighbors, your family, and your church. When you experience God's presence and invite His Son into your heart, you feel the need to share His message and to obey His commandments. God loved this world so much that He sent His Son to save it. Living in response to His perfect love is our privilege and our new nature in Him.

MORE PROMISES FROM GOD'S WORD

If you love me, you will obey what I command.

John 14:15 NIV

We love Him because He first loved us.

1 John 4:19 NKJV

And we know that in all things God works for the good of those who love him, who have been called according to his purpose.

Romans 8:28 NIV

It is good to praise the LORD and make music to your name, O Most High, to proclaim your love in the morning and your faithfulness at night....

Psalm 92:1-2 NIV

If I speak the languages of men and of angels, but do not have love, I am a sounding gong or a clanging cymbal.

1 Corinthians 13:1 HCSB

MORE GREAT IDEAS

God loves each of us as if there were only one of us.

St. Augustine

The fact is, God no longer deals with us in judgment but in mercy. If people got what they deserved, this old planet would have ripped apart at the seams centuries ago. Praise God that because of His great love "we are not consumed, for his compassions never fail" (Lam. 3:22).

Joni Eareckson Tada

Accepting God's love as a gift instead of trying to earn it had somehow seemed presumptuous and arrogant to me, when, in fact, my pride was tricking me into thinking that I could merit His love and forgiveness with my own strength.

Lisa Whelchel

Being loved by Him whose opinion matters most gives us the security to risk loving, too—even loving ourselves.

Gloria Gaither

God is a God of unconditional,
unremitting love,
a love that corrects and chastens
but never ceases.

—

Kay Arthur

Our Savior kneels down and gazes upon
the darkest acts of our lives.
But rather than recoil in horror,
he reaches out in kindness and says,
"I can clean that if you want."
And from the basin of his grace, he scoops
a palm full of mercy and washes our sin.

—

Max Lucado

A PRAYER FOR TODAY

Dear Lord, thank You for loving me. And thank
You for sending Your Son Jesus to this earth so that
I can receive Your gift of eternal love and eternal
life. I praise You today, Dear God. Amen

YOUR OWN THOUGHTS ABOUT
ACCEPTING GOD'S LOVE

CHAPTER 11

REDEEMED FROM THE WORLD'S PRESSURES

*Do not love the world or the things
that belong to the world.
If anyone loves the world,
love for the Father is not in him.*

—

1 John 2:15 HCSB

We live in the world, but we should not worship it—yet at every turn, or so it seems, we are tempted to do otherwise. The 21st-century world in which we live is a noisy, distracting place, a place that offers countless temptations and dangers. The world seems to cry, "Worship me with your time, your money, your energy, your stuff, your thoughts, and your life!" But if we are led by the Spirit, we won't fall prey to that temptation.

Because you've been redeemed by God, you don't have to give in to the temptations and distractions of modern-day society. As children of God, we realize that He will always provide a way of escape so that we can stand up under the pressure of this world.

> Our joy ends where love of the world begins.
>
> —
>
> *C. H. Spurgeon*

C. S. Lewis said, "Aim at heaven and you will get earth thrown in; aim at earth and you will get neither." That's good advice. You're likely to hit what you aim at, so aim high . . . aim at heaven. When we focus our attention on Jesus, the things of this earth will grow strangely dim in the light of His glory and grace.

MORE PROMISES FROM GOD'S WORD

Pure and undefiled religion before our God and Father is this: to look after orphans and widows in their distress and to keep oneself unstained by the world.

James 1:27 HCSB

No one should deceive himself. If anyone among you thinks he is wise in this age, he must become foolish so that he can become wise. For the wisdom of this world is foolishness with God, since it is written: He catches the wise in their craftiness.

1 Corinthians 3:18-19 HCSB

So do not worry, saying, "What shall we eat?" or "What shall we drink?" or "What shall we wear?" For the pagans run after all these things, and your heavenly Father knows that you need them. But seek first his kingdom and his righteousness, and all these things will be given to you as well. Therefore do not worry about tomorrow, for tomorrow will worry about itself. Each day has enough trouble of its own.

Matthew 6:31-34 NIV

MORE GREAT IDEAS

The only ultimate disaster that can befall us, I have come to realize, is to feel ourselves to be home on earth.

Max Lucado

The true Christian, though he is in revolt against the world's efforts to brainwash him, is no mere rebel for rebellion's sake. He dissents from the world because he knows that it cannot make good on its promises.

A. W. Tozer

Every day, I find countless opportunities to decide whether I will obey God and demonstrate my love for Him or try to please myself or the world system. God is waiting for my choices.

Bill Bright

As you separate yourself from worldly things and saturate yourself with Scripture, that which is good will increasingly replace that which is evil.

John MacArthur

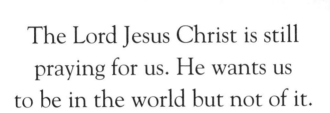

The Lord Jesus Christ is still
praying for us. He wants us
to be in the world but not of it.

—

Charles Stanley

A TIMELY TIP

The world's value system is flawed. God's value system is not.

A PRAYER FOR TODAY

Dear Lord, turn my eyes from looking to the world for approval. Today, Father, help me focus less on the world and more on You. Amen

YOUR OWN THOUGHTS ABOUT BEING *IN* THE WORLD BUT NOT *OF* THE WORLD

CHAPTER 12

REDEEMED
AND AT PEACE

*The peace of God, which passeth
all understanding, shall keep your hearts
and minds through Christ Jesus.*

—

Philippians 4:7 KJV

Our world is in a state of constant change and so are we. God is not. At times, everything around us seems to be changing: we're growing up; we are growing older; loved ones pass on. Sometimes, the world seems to be trembling beneath our feet. But we can be comforted in the knowledge that our Heavenly Father is the rock that cannot be shaken.

Perhaps you seek a new direction or a sense of renewed purpose, but those feelings should never rob you of the genuine peace that can and should be yours through a personal relationship with Jesus. The demands of everyday living should never obscure the fact that Christ died so that you might have life abundant and eternal.

Have you found the lasting peace that can be yours through Jesus, or are you still rushing after the illusion of "peace and happiness" that our world promises but cannot deliver? The world's "peace" is fleeting; Christ's peace is forever.

Christ is standing at the door, waiting patiently for you to invite Him to rule your heart. His eternal peace is offered freely. Claim it today.

MORE PROMISES FROM GOD'S WORD

God has called us to live in peace.

1 Corinthians 7:15 NIV

And let the peace of God rule in your hearts . . . and be ye thankful.

Colossians 3:15 KJV

You will keep in perfect peace him whose mind is steadfast, because he trusts in you.

Isaiah 26:3 NIV

I have told you these things, so that in me you may have peace. In this world you will have trouble. But take heart! I have overcome the world.

John 16:33 NIV

For He is our peace.

Ephesians 2:14 HCSB

MORE GREAT IDEAS

God's peace is like a river, not a pond. In other words, a sense of health and well-being, both of which are expressions of the Hebrew *shalom*, can permeate our homes even when we're in white-water rapids.

Beth Moore

What peace can they have who are not at peace with God?

Matthew Henry

When you and I are related to Jesus Christ, our strength and wisdom and peace and joy and love and hope may run out, but His life rushes in to keep us filled to the brim. We are showered with blessings, not because of anything we have or have not done, but simply because of Him.

Anne Graham Lotz

That peace, which has been described and which believers enjoy, is a participation of the peace which their glorious Lord and Master himself enjoys.

Jonathan Edwards

Peace is the deepest thing
a human personality can know;
it is almighty.

—

Oswald Chambers

God has promised us abundance, peace, and eternal life. These treasures are ours for the asking; all we must do is claim them. One of the great mysteries of life is why on earth do so many of us wait so very long to claim them?

Marie T. Freeman

We're prone to want God to change our circumstances, but He wants to change our character. We think that peace comes from the outside in, but it comes from the inside out.

Warren Wiersbe

God is in control of history; it's His story. Doesn't that give you a great peace—especially when world events seem so tumultuous and insane?

Kay Arthur

The fruit of our placing all things in God's hands is the presence of His abiding peace in our hearts.

Hannah Whitall Smith

A TIMELY TIP

God's peace surpasses human understanding. When you accept His peace, it will revolutionize your life.

A PRAYER FOR TODAY

Dear Lord, I will open my heart to You. And I thank You, God, for Your love, for Your peace, and for Your Son. Amen

YOUR OWN THOUGHTS ABOUT
FINDING PEACE

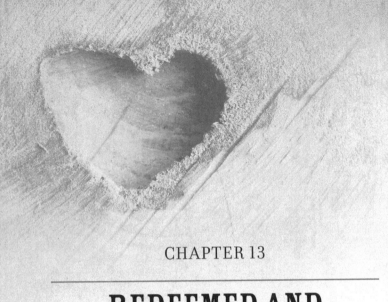

CHAPTER 13

REDEEMED AND COURAGEOUS

Be strong and courageous, and do the work. Don't be afraid or discouraged, for the Lord God, my God, is with you. He won't leave you or forsake you.

—

1 Chronicles 28:20 HCSB

Every human life is a tapestry of events: some grand, some not-so-grand, and some downright disheartening. When we reach the mountaintops of life, praising God is easy. In our moments of triumph, we trust God's plan. But, when the storm clouds form overhead and we find ourselves in the dark valley of despair, our faith is stretched, sometimes to the breaking point. As Christians, we can be comforted: Wherever we find ourselves, whether at the top of the mountain or the depths of the valley, God is there, and because He cares for us, we can live courageously.

Believing Christians have every reason to be courageous. After all, the ultimate battle has already been fought and won on the cross at Calvary. But, even dedicated followers of Christ may find their courage tested by the inevitable disappointments and tragedies that occur in the lives of believers and nonbelievers alike.

The next time you find your courage tested to the limit, remember that God is as near as your next

> Dreaming the dream of God is not for cowards.
>
> —
>
> *Joey Johnson*

breath, and that He offers salvation to His children. He is your shield and your strength; He is your protector and your deliverer. Call upon Him in your hour of need and then be comforted. Whatever your challenge, whatever your trouble, God can handle it.

There comes a time
when we simply have to face
the challenges in our lives
and stop backing down.

—

John Eldredge

MORE PROMISES FROM GOD'S WORD

For God has not given us a spirit of fearfulness, but one of power, love, and sound judgment.

2 Timothy 1:7 HCSB

Be alert, stand firm in the faith, be brave and strong.

1 Corinthians 16:13 HCSB

Haven't I commanded you: be strong and courageous? Do not be afraid or discouraged, for the Lord your God is with you wherever you go.

Joshua 1:9 HCSB

But when Jesus heard it, He answered him, "Don't be afraid. Only believe."

Luke 8:50 HCSB

But He said to them, "Why are you fearful, you of little faith?" Then He got up and rebuked the winds and the sea. And there was a great calm.

Matthew 8:26 HCSB

MORE GREAT IDEAS

Daniel looked into the face of God and would not fear the face of a lion.

C. H. Spurgeon

Jesus Christ can make the weakest man into a divine dreadnought, fearing nothing.

Oswald Chambers

Why rely on yourself and fall? Cast yourself upon His arm. Be not afraid. He will not let you slip. Cast yourself in confidence. He will receive you and heal you.

St. Augustine

Perhaps I am stronger than I think.

Thomas Merton

The truth of Christ brings assurance and so removes the former problem of fear and uncertainty.

A. W. Tozer

> Faith looks back and draws courage;
> hope looks ahead and keeps desire alive.
>
> —
>
> *John Eldredge*

A PRAYER FOR TODAY

Lord, sometimes I am afraid. Please give me courage. Let me be courageous, faith-filled, and keep me mindful that, with You as my protector, I am secure throughout eternity. Amen

YOUR OWN THOUGHTS ABOUT
LIVING COURAGEOUSLY

CHAPTER 14

REDEEMED AND PROTECTED

*The Lord is my rock,
my fortress, and my deliverer.*

—

Psalm 18:2 HCSB

In a world filled with more frustrations than we can count, God's Son offers the ultimate peace. God has promised to protect us, and He intends to fulfill His promise. In a world filled with dangers and temptations, God is the ultimate armor. In a world filled with misleading messages, God's Word is the ultimate truth.

Have you ever faced challenges that seemed too big to handle? Have you ever faced big problems that, despite your best efforts, simply could not be solved? If so, you know how uncomfortable it is to feel helpless in the face of difficult circumstances. Thankfully, even when there's nowhere else to turn, you can turn your thoughts and prayers to God, and He will respond.

God's hand uplifts those who turn their hearts and prayers to Him. Count yourself among that number. When you do, you can live courageously and joyfully, knowing that "this too will pass"—but that God's love for you will not. And you can draw strength from the knowledge that you are a marvelous creation, loved, protected, and uplifted by the knowledge that you are redeemed by a loving heavenly Father. Today, accept God's peace and wear God's armor against the dangers of our world.

MORE PROMISES FROM GOD'S WORD

Finally, my brethren, be strong in the Lord and in the power of His might. Put on the whole armor of God, that you may be able to stand against the wiles of the devil.

Ephesians 6:10-11 NKJV

The Lord your God in your midst, The Mighty One, will save; He will rejoice over you with gladness, He will quiet you with His love, He will rejoice over you with singing.

Zephaniah 3:17 NKJV

Those who trust the Lord are like Mount Zion, which sits unmoved forever. As the mountains surround Jerusalem, the Lord surrounds his people now and forever.

Psalm 125:1-2 NCV

But the Lord will be a refuge for His people.

Joel 3:16 HCSB

MORE GREAT IDEAS

Prayer is our pathway not only to divine protection, but also to a personal, intimate relationship with God.

Shirley Dobson

He goes before us, follows behind us, and hems us safe inside the realm of His protection.

Beth Moore

We can take great comfort that God never sleeps—so we can.

Dianna Booher

It is faith that what happens to me matters to God as well as to me that gives me joy, that promises me that I am eternally the subject of God's compassion, and that assures me that the compassion was manifested most brilliantly when God came to us in a stable in Bethlehem.

Madeleine L'Engle

The Lord God of heaven and earth, the Almighty Creator of all things, He who holds the universe in His hand as though it were a very little thing, He is your Shepherd, and He has charged Himself with the care and keeping of you, as a shepherd is charged with the care and keeping of his sheep.

Hannah Whitall Smith

It is an act of the will to allow God to be our refuge. Otherwise we live outside of his love and protection, wondering why we feel alone and afraid.

Mary Morrison Suggs

Under heaven's lock and key, we are protected by the most efficient security system available: the power of God.

Charles Swindoll

The Will of God will never take you where the Grace of God will not protect you.

Anonymous

A TIMELY TIP

If you'd like infinite protection, there's only one place you can receive it: from an infinite God.

A PRAYER FOR TODAY

Lord, You are my Shepherd. You care for me; You comfort me; You watch over me; and You have redeemed me. I will praise You, Father, for Your glorious works, for Your protection, for Your love, and for Your Son. Amen

YOUR OWN THOUGHTS ABOUT
THE NEED FOR GOD'S PROTECTION

CHAPTER 15

REDEEMED

My lips will shout for joy
when I sing praise to You,
because You have redeemed me.

—

Psalm 71:23 HCSB

Christ came to this earth for a purpose: to redeem a fallen world. God sent His Son to redeem us from every shortcoming, from every failure, from every sin. He shed His blood and suffered—for you. He endured unspeakable pain—for you. He willingly endured humiliation and torture—for you. He conquered death and rose in victory—for you.

Christ was never double-minded. He lived and died and rose again with a clear purpose in mind: so that through His sacrifice, the world might be transformed. Today, Jesus stands at the door and knocks. He is offering to walk with you through this life and throughout all eternity. He is offering to wash away your sins and give you a new life in Him. He is offering you a priceless treasure. So, as you approach Jesus today in prayer, think about His sacrifice, His grace, and His purpose—the things He did that we cannot. He came to this earth so that you, and all of us, might receive the gift we cannot earn and only He can give—to be redeemed.

> My lips will shout for joy when I sing praise to You, because You have redeemed me.
>
> —
>
> *Psalm 71:23 HCSB*

MORE PROMISES FROM GOD'S WORD

But when the completion of the time came, God sent His Son, born of a woman, born under the law, to redeem those under the law, so that we might receive adoption as sons.

Galatians 4:4-5 HCSB

My soul, praise the Lord, and do not forget all His benefits. He forgives all your sin; He heals all your diseases. He redeems your life from the Pit; He crowns you with faithful love and compassion.

Psalm 103:2-4 HCSB

But God's mercy is great, and he loved us very much. Though we were spiritually dead because of the things we did against God, he gave us new life with Christ. You have been saved by God's grace.

Ephesians 2:4-5 NCV

But God demonstrates His own love toward us, in that while we were still sinners, Christ died for us.

Romans 5:8 NKJV

MORE GREAT IDEAS

There was no other way for sin's penalty to be paid and for us to be redeemed. The Cross is the measure of God's love.

Billy Graham

Redeemed, how I love to proclaim it! Redeemed by the blood of the Lamb; Redeemed through His infinite mercy, His child, and forever, I am.

Fanny Crosby

Mistakes offer the possibility for redemption and a new start in God's kingdom. No matter what you're guilty of, God can restore your innocence.

Barbara Johnson

Jesus Christ rose from the dead to give believers the assurance of forgiveness—a vital part of the gospel of Christ.

Charles Stanley

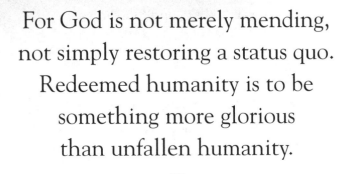

For God is not merely mending,
not simply restoring a status quo.
Redeemed humanity is to be
something more glorious
than unfallen humanity.

—

C. S. Lewis

> Nothing can ever change God
> or the reality of redemption.
> Base your faith on that, and you are as
> eternally secure as God Himself.
>
> —
>
> *Oswald Chambers*

A PRAYER FOR TODAY

Dear Lord, I thank You for the love You have shown me and for the blessings You have given me. Your Son died and rose again so that I might be redeemed. I am truly humbled by His sacrifice. I will praise You today, tomorrow, and forever, Father, for Your love, for Your mercy, and for Your Son. Amen

YOUR OWN THOUGHTS ABOUT
THE REDEEMING POWER OF CHRIST

CHAPTER 16

REDEEMED AND PUTTING GOD FIRST

Do not have other gods besides Me.

—

Exodus 20:3 HCSB

Is God your top priority? Have you given His Son your heart, your soul, your talents, and your time? The answers to these questions will determine how you prioritize your days and your life.

As you think about your own relationship with God, remember this: all of mankind is engaged in the practice of worship. Some people choose to worship God and, as a result, experience the redemption and joy that He intends for His children. Other people distance themselves from God by worshiping such things as earthly possessions or personal gratification.

In the book of Exodus, God warns that we should place no gods before Him. Yet, we often place our Lord in second, third, or fourth place.

When we place our desires for the things of the world above our love for God, we choose second best, at best, and miss the chance to experience God's glory at its fullest. Choose God this day as your first priority and live in hope and strength.

> When all else is gone, God is still left. Nothing changes Him.
>
> —
>
> *Hannah Whitall Smith*

MORE PROMISES FROM GOD'S WORD

Jesus answered, "'Love the Lord your God with all your heart, all your soul, and all your mind.' This is the first and most important command."

Matthew 22:37-38 NCV

God is Spirit, and those who worship Him must worship in spirit and truth.

John 4:24 HCSB

Then Jesus said to His disciples, "If anyone wants to come with Me, he must deny himself, take up his cross, and follow Me."

Matthew 16:24 HCSB

Let the words of my mouth and the meditation of my heart be acceptable in Your sight, O Lord, my strength and my Redeemer.

Psalm 19:14 NKJV

MORE GREAT IDEAS

I can see how it might be possible for a man to look down upon the earth and be an atheist, but I cannot conceive how he could look up into the heavens and say there is no God.

Abraham Lincoln

One with God is a majority.

Billy Graham

Huge as this universe is, God has complete power over it, as you have with a ball which you toss in your hand.

C. H. Spurgeon

Our concepts of measurement embrace mountains and men, atoms and stars, gravity, energy, numbers, speed, but never God. We cannot speak of measure or amount or size or weight and at the same time be speaking of God, for these tell of degrees and there are no degrees in God. All that he is he is without growth or addition or development.

A. W. Tozer

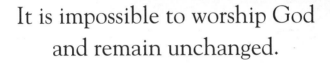

It is impossible to worship God
and remain unchanged.

—

Henry Blackaby

Jesus Christ is the first and last, author and finisher, beginning and end, alpha and omega, and by Him all other things hold together. He must be first or nothing. God never comes next!

—

Vance Havner

A PRAYER FOR TODAY

Dear Lord, keep me mindful of the need to place You first in every aspect of my life. You have blessed me beyond measure, Father, and I will praise You with my thoughts, my prayers, my testimony, and my service, this day and every day. Amen

YOUR OWN THOUGHTS ABOUT
PUTTING GOD FIRST IN YOUR LIFE

CHAPTER 17

REDEEMED BY HOPE

*Let us hold on to the confession
of our hope without wavering,
for He who promised is faithful.*

—

Hebrews 10:23 HCSB

When times are tough, we may be confronted with the illusion of hopelessness. Try though we might, we simply can't envision a solution to our problems. During these times, we may question God—His love, His presence, even His very existence. Despite God's promises, despite Christ's love, and despite our many blessings, we may envision little or no hope for the future.

If you find yourself falling into the spiritual traps of worry and discouragement, seek the encouraging words of fellow Christians, and the healing touch of Jesus. After all, it was Christ who promised, "These things I have spoken unto you, that in me ye might have peace. In the world ye shall have tribulation: but be of good cheer; I have overcome the world" (John 16:33 KJV).

Because you have been redeemed, have hope for the future. After all, your troubles are temporary, but heaven lasts forever. Place your future into the hands of a loving and all-knowing God. You can live amid the uncertainties of today, knowing that God has dominion over all your tomorrows. Trust God in good times and hard times and be both wise and blessed.

MORE PROMISES FROM GOD'S WORD

Hope deferred makes the heart sick.

Proverbs 13:12 NKJV

Sustain me as You promised, and I will live; do not let me be ashamed of my hope.

Psalm 119:116 HCSB

For I know the thoughts that I think toward you, says the Lord, thoughts of peace and not of evil, to give you a future and a hope. Then you will call upon Me and go and pray to Me, and I will listen to you.

Jeremiah 29:11-12 NKJV

Be of good courage, and He shall strengthen your heart, all you who hope in the Lord.

Psalm 31:24 NKJV

I wait for the Lord; I wait, and put my hope in His word.

Psalm 130:5 HCSB

MORE GREAT IDEAS

Hope is nothing more than the expectation of those things which faith has believed to be truly promised by God.

John Calvin

Faith looks back and draws courage; hope looks ahead and keeps desire alive.

John Eldredge

The hope we have in Jesus is the anchor for the soul—something sure and steadfast, preventing drifting or giving way, lowered to the depth of God's love.

Franklin Graham

It may be that the day of judgment will dawn tomorrow; in that case, we shall gladly stop working for a better tomorrow. But not before.

Dietrich Bonhoeffer

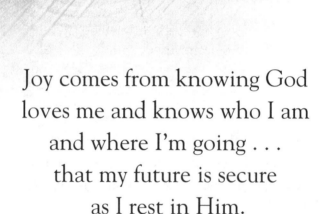

Joy comes from knowing God
loves me and knows who I am
and where I'm going . . .
that my future is secure
as I rest in Him.

—

James Dobson

A TIMELY TIP

Never be afraid to hope—or to ask—for a miracle.

A PRAYER FOR TODAY

Dear Lord, let my hopes begin and end with You. When I am discouraged, let me turn to You. When I am weak, let me find strength in You. You are my Father, and I will place my faith, my trust, and my hopes in You. Amen

YOUR OWN THOUGHTS ABOUT
YOUR HOPE FOR THE FUTURE

CHAPTER 18

REDEEMED AND JOYFUL

*This is the day the Lord has made;
let us rejoice and be glad in it.*

—

Psalm 118:24 HCSB

Being redeemed brings the opportunity to experience incredible joy. Yet sometimes, amid the inevitable hustle and bustle of life here on earth, you may lose sight of your blessings as you wrestle with the challenges of everyday life.

Joy, however, is not determined by your circumstances. Joy comes from the Lord. Being in the Lord can keep you mindful of that joy—love God and His Son; depend upon God for strength; follow God's will; and strive to obey His Holy Word.

A life of intimacy with God is characterized by joy.

—

Oswald Chambers

As you embark upon the next phase of your journey, celebrate the life that God has given you. Your Creator has blessed you beyond measure. Honor Him with your prayers, your words, your deeds, and experience the joy only He can give.

MORE PROMISES FROM GOD'S WORD

But let all who take refuge in You rejoice.

Psalm 5:11 HCSB

Delight yourself also in the Lord, and He shall give you the desires of your heart.

Psalm 37:4 NKJV

Rejoice in the Lord, you righteous ones; praise from the upright is beautiful.

Psalm 33:1 HCSB

Weeping may endure for a night, but joy comes in the morning.

Psalm 30:5 NKJV

Rejoice in the Lord always. I will say it again: Rejoice!

Philippians 4:4 HCSB

MORE GREAT IDEAS

I choose joy. I will refuse the temptation to be cynical; cynicism is the tool of a lazy thinker. I will refuse to see people as anything less than human beings, created by God. I will refuse to see any problem as anything less than an opportunity to see God.

Max Lucado

Some of us seem so anxious about avoiding hell that we forget to celebrate our journey toward heaven.

Philip Yancey

The Christian should be an alleluia from head to foot!

St. Augustine

The Christian lifestyle is not one of legalistic do's and don'ts, but one that is positive, attractive, and joyful.

Vonette Bright

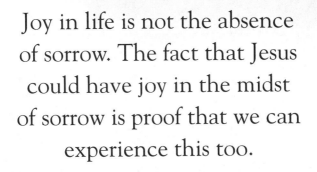

Joy in life is not the absence
of sorrow. The fact that Jesus
could have joy in the midst
of sorrow is proof that we can
experience this too.

—

Warren Wiersbe

A TIMELY TIP

Identify, meditate on, and respond to the many reasons God has given you to rejoice today.

A PRAYER FOR TODAY

Dear Lord, You have given me so many blessings; let me celebrate Your gifts. I praise You, Father, for the gift of redemption through Your Son. Make me joyful and let that joy shine for all to see. Amen

YOUR OWN THOUGHTS ABOUT
BEING JOYFUL AND SHARING THAT JOY

CHAPTER 19

REDEEMED FOR A PURPOSE

For it is God who is working among you both the willing and the working for His good purpose.

—

Philippians 2:13 HCSB

God has a plan for your life—a plan that is near and dear to His heart. A purpose, like everything else in the universe, that begins in the heart of God. Whether you realize it or not, God has a direction for your life.

The writer of Proverbs says, "The heart of man plans his way, but the Lord establishes His steps" (Proverbs 16:9, ESV). The Holy Spirit is moving in you, setting your path, guiding you daily toward the purpose He has in store for you.

Sometimes, God's intentions will be clear to you. At other times, you may find yourself searching for the direction of your next step. But, even on those difficult days when you are unsure which way to turn, keep sight of the fact that God created you for a reason. Walk in His love even when the path isn't always clear, confident that He knows the way.

> God is more concerned with the direction of your life than with its speed.
>
> —
>
> *Marie T. Freeman*

MORE PROMISES FROM GOD'S WORD

We know that all things work together for the good of those who love God: those who are called according to His purpose.

Romans 8:28 HCSB

I will instruct you and show you the way to go; with My eye on you, I will give counsel.

Psalm 32:8 HCSB

You reveal the path of life to me; in Your presence is abundant joy; in Your right hand are eternal pleasures.

Psalm 16:11 HCSB

Commit your activities to the Lord and your plans will be achieved.

Proverbs 16:3 HCSB

To everything there is a season, a time for every purpose under heaven.

Ecclesiastes 3:1 NKJV

MORE GREAT IDEAS

Nothing can reach us, from any source in earth or hell, no matter how evil, which God cannot turn to His own redemptive purpose. Let us be glad that the way is not a game of chance—it is a way appointed for God's eternal glory and our final good.

Elisabeth Elliot

When God speaks to you through the Bible, prayer, circumstances, the church, or in some other way, he has a purpose in mind for your life.

Henry Blackaby and Claude King

Without God, life has no purpose, and without purpose, life has no meaning.

Rick Warren

Whatever purpose motivates your life, it must be something big enough and grand enough to make the investment worthwhile.

Warren Wiersbe

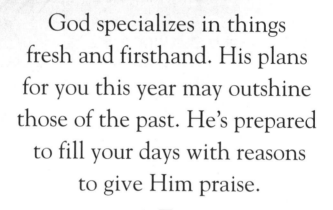

God specializes in things
fresh and firsthand. His plans
for you this year may outshine
those of the past. He's prepared
to fill your days with reasons
to give Him praise.

—

Joni Eareckson Tada

A TIMELY TIP

God has a plan for your life. Pray for God's guidance and follow wherever He leads.

A PRAYER FOR TODAY

Lord, thank You for the purpose You have for my life. Give me Your blessings and lead me along a path that is pleasing to You. Amen

YOUR OWN THOUGHTS ABOUT
GOD'S PURPOSE FOR YOUR LIFE

CHAPTER 20

REDEEMED FROM THE FIGHT THAT'S ALREADY BEEN WON

*And we have seen and testify
that the Father has sent his Son
to be the Savior of the world.*

—

1 John 4:14 NIV

There's nothing anyone can do to become redeemed. God has already done it. How marvelous it is that God's Son walked among us. Had He not chosen to do so, we might feel removed from a distant Creator. But ours is not a distant God. Ours is a God who understands far better than we ever could the essence of what it means to be human.

God understands our hopes, our fears, and our temptations. He understands what it means to be angry and what it costs to forgive. He knows the heart, the conscience, and the soul of every person who has ever lived, including you.

> Our salvation comes to us so easily because it cost God so much.
>
> —
>
> *Oswald Chambers*

Christ sacrificed His life on the cross so that we might have eternal life. This gift, freely given by God's only begotten Son, is the priceless possession of everyone who accepts Him as Lord and Savior. God is waiting patiently for each of us to accept the gift of eternal life. May we claim Christ's gift and share His message with the world.

It is by God's grace that we have been saved, through faith. We are saved not because of our good deeds but because of our faith in Christ. May we, who have been given so much, praise our Savior for the gift of salvation, and may we share the joyous news of our Master's love and His grace.

It is by the name of Jesus Christ of Nazareth . . . Salvation is found in no one else, for there is no other name under heaven given to men by which we must be saved.

—

Acts 4:10, 12 NIV

MORE PROMISES FROM GOD'S WORD

Blessed be the God and Father of our Lord Jesus Christ, who according to His great mercy has caused us to be born again to a living hope through the resurrection of Jesus Christ from the dead.

1 Peter 1:3 NASB

Here is a trustworthy saying that deserves full acceptance: Christ Jesus came into the world to save sinners—of whom I am the worst.

1 Timothy 1:15 NIV

The sun will be turned into darkness, and the moon will turn bloodred, before that great and glorious day of the Lord arrives. And anyone who calls on the name of the Lord will be saved.

Acts 2:20-21 NLT

But if from there you seek the LORD your God, you will find him if you look for him with all your heart and with all your soul.

Deuteronomy 4:29 NIV

MORE GREAT IDEAS

Personal salvation is not an occasional rendezvous with Deity; it is an actual dwelling with God.

Billy Graham

God's goal is not to make you happy. It is to make you His.

Max Lucado

There is no detour to holiness. Jesus came to the resurrection through the cross, not around it.

Leighton Ford

Today is the day of salvation. Some people miss heaven by only eighteen inches—the distance between their heads and their hearts.

Corrie ten Boom

Do we so appreciate the marvelous salvation of Jesus Christ that we are our utmost for His highest?

Oswald Chambers

We're not only saved by grace,
but the Bible says we're sustained by grace.

—

Bill Hybels

A PRAYER FOR TODAY

Dear Lord, I am only here on this earth for a brief while. But, You have offered me the priceless gift of eternal life through Your Son Jesus. I accept Your gift, Lord, with thanksgiving and praise. Let me share the Good News with all those who need Your healing touch. Amen

YOUR OWN THOUGHTS ABOUT
CHRIST'S SACRIFICE FOR YOU

CHAPTER 21

REDEEMED BY GRACE

*For all have sinned and fall short
of the glory of God, and are justified
freely by his grace through the redemption
that came by Christ Jesus.*

—

Romans 3:23-24 NIV

God's grace is not earned . . . thank goodness! To earn God's love and His gift of eternal life would be far beyond the abilities of even the most righteous guys, girls, men, or women. Grace is not an earthly reward for righteous behavior; it is an amazing spiritual gift which can be accepted through Christ.

God's grace is the ultimate gift, releasing in us a response of thanksgiving. Praise the Creator for His priceless gift!

Have you thanked God today for blessings that are too numerous to count? Have you offered Him your heartfelt prayers and your wholehearted praise? If not, it's time to slow down and offer a prayer of thanksgiving to the One who has given you life on earth and life eternal. No matter your circumstances, thank the Lord today for His unspeakable gift of grace.

> Grace is an outrageous blessing bestowed freely on a totally undeserving recipient.
>
> —
>
> *Bill Hybels*

MORE PROMISES FROM GOD'S WORD

For the law was given through Moses; grace and truth came through Jesus Christ.

John 1:17 NIV

In Him we have redemption through His blood, the forgiveness of sins, according to the riches of His grace which He made to abound toward us in all wisdom and prudence....

Ephesians 1:7-8 NKJV

For it is by grace you have been saved, through faith—and this not from yourselves, it is the gift of God—not by works, so that no one can boast.

Ephesians 2:8-9 NIV

Let us then approach the throne of grace with confidence, so that we may receive mercy and find grace to help us in our time of need.

Hebrews 4:16 NIV

MORE GREAT IDEAS

The grace of God is sufficient for all our needs, for every problem, and for every difficulty, for every broken heart, and for every human sorrow.

Peter Marshall

To believe is to take freely what God gives freely.

C. H. Spurgeon

The grace of God is infinite and eternal. As it had no beginning, so it can have no end, and being an attribute of God, it is as boundless as infinitude.

A. W. Tozer

If you are a believer, your judgment will not determine your eternal destiny. Christ's finished work on Calvary was applied to you the moment you accepted Christ as Savior.

Beth Moore

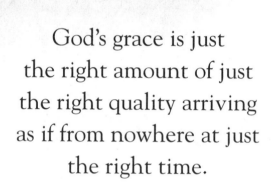

God's grace is just
the right amount of just
the right quality arriving
as if from nowhere at just
the right time.

—

Bill Bright

All praise to our redeeming Lord, who joins us by His grace and bids us, each to each restored, together seek His face.

—

Charles Wesley

A PRAYER FOR TODAY

Lord, You have redeemed me. Keep me mindful that Your grace is a gift that I can accept but cannot earn. I praise You for that priceless gift. Let me share Your good news with a world that desperately needs Your healing touch. Amen

YOUR OWN THOUGHTS ABOUT
THE GIFT OF GOD'S GRACE

CHAPTER 22

REDEEMED AND CONTENT

*But godliness with contentment
is a great gain.*

—

1 Timothy 6:6 HCSB

Everywhere we turn, or so it seems, the world promises us contentment and happiness. But the contentment that the world offers is fleeting and incomplete. Thankfully, the contentment that God offers is all encompassing and everlasting.

Happiness depends less upon our circumstances than upon our thoughts. When we turn our thoughts to God, to His gifts, and to His glorious creation, we experience the joy that God intends for His children. But, when we focus on the negative aspects of life—or when we disobey God's commandments—we cause ourselves needless suffering.

> Real contentment hinges on what's happening inside us, not around us.
>
> —
>
> *Charles Stanley*

Do you sincerely want to be content? Set your mind and your heart upon God's love and His grace. The fullness of life in Christ is available to all who seek it and claim it. Give thanks for God's redemption, and then claim the joy, the contentment, and the spiritual abundance that the Lord offers you.

MORE PROMISES FROM GOD'S WORD

I have learned to be content in whatever circumstances I am.

Philippians 4:11 HCSB

The LORD will give strength to His people; the LORD will bless His people with peace.

Psalm 29:11 NKJV

Let your conduct be without covetousness; be content with such things as you have. For He Himself has said, "I will never leave you nor forsake you."

Hebrews 13:5 NKJV

Take My yoke upon you and learn from Me, because I am gentle and humble in heart, and you will find rest for your souls. For My yoke is easy and My burden is light.

Matthew 11:29-30 HCSB

MORE GREAT IDEAS

I believe that in every time and place it is within our power to acquiesce in the will of God—and what peace it brings to do so!

Elisabeth Elliot

Father and Mother lived on the edge of poverty, and yet their contentment was not dependent upon their surroundings. Their relationship to each other and to the Lord gave them strength and happiness.

Corrie ten Boom

Contentment is possible when we stop striving for more.

Charles Swindoll

Nobody who gets enough food and clothing in a world where most are hungry and cold has any business to talk about "misery."

C. S. Lewis

When we do what is right,
we have contentment,
peace, and happiness.

—

Beverly LaHaye

A TIMELY TIP

Be content where you are, even if it's not exactly where you want to end up. Be patient and trust God.

A PRAYER FOR TODAY

Dear Lord, You offer me contentment and peace; let me accept Your peace. Help me to trust Your Word, to follow Your commandments, and to welcome the peace of Jesus into my heart. Amen

YOUR OWN THOUGHTS ABOUT FINDING CONTENTMENT

CHAPTER 23

REDEEMED TO SERVE

If anyone serves Me, let him follow Me;
and where I am, there My servant will
be also. If anyone serves Me,
him My Father will honor.

—

John 12:26 NKJV

Because you've been redeemed, your life has purpose. That purpose is often revealed through service to God and others. As Paul writes to the church in Galatia, "For you were called to freedom, brothers. Only do not use your freedom as an opportunity for the flesh, but through love serve one another. For the whole law is fulfilled in one word: 'You shall love your neighbor as yourself'" (Galatians 5:13-14, ESV). Let whatever your path, whatever your calling, whatever your passion, whatever it is that you feel led to do, center around serving God.

Jesus was the ultimate servant, the Savior who gave His life for mankind. He teaches us that the most esteemed men and women are the humblest of servants.

> In Jesus, the service of God and the service of the least of the brethren were one.
>
> —
>
> *Dietrich Bonhoeffer*

Today, serve your neighbors. Find a need and fill it. Lend a helping hand and share a word of kindness. Experience the heart of God through your service and glorify God in the doing of it.

MORE PROMISES FROM GOD'S WORD

Worship the Lord your God and . . . serve Him only.

Matthew 4:10 HCSB

A person should consider us in this way: as servants of Christ and managers of God's mysteries. In this regard, it is expected of managers that each one be found faithful.

1 Corinthians 4:1-2 HCSB

If they serve Him obediently, they will end their days in prosperity and their years in happiness.

Job 36:11 HCSB

We must do the works of Him who sent Me while it is day. Night is coming when no one can work.

John 9:4 HCSB

Serve the Lord with gladness.

Psalm 100:2 HCSB

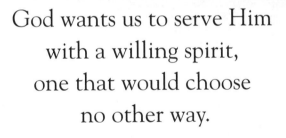

God wants us to serve Him
with a willing spirit,
one that would choose
no other way.

—

Beth Moore

MORE GREAT IDEAS

Every tiny bit of my life that has value I owe to the redemption of Jesus Christ. Am I doing anything to enable Him to bring His redemption into evident reality in the lives of others?

Oswald Chambers

When you're enjoying the fulfillment and fellowship that inevitably accompanies authentic service, ministry is a joy. Instead of exhausting you, it energizes you; instead of burnout, you experience blessing.

Bill Hybels

You can judge how far you have risen in the scale of life by asking one question: How wisely and how deeply do I care? To be Christianized is to be sensitized. Christians are people who care.

E. Stanley Jones

In God's family, there is to be one great body of people: servants. In fact, that's the way to the top in his kingdom.

Charles Swindoll

No life can surpass that of a man who quietly
continues to serve God in the place
where providence has placed him.

—

C. H. Spurgeon

A PRAYER FOR TODAY

Dear Lord, give me a servant's heart. When Jesus humbled Himself and became a servant, He also became an example for His followers. Make me a faithful steward of my gifts, and let me share with those in need. Amen

YOUR OWN THOUGHTS ABOUT
SERVING OTHERS IN GOD'S NAME

CHAPTER 24

REDEEMED
AND THANKFUL

Enter into His gates with thanksgiving,
and into His courts with praise.
Be thankful to Him, and bless His name.
For the Lord is good;
His mercy is everlasting, and His truth
endures to all generations.

—

Psalm 100:4-5 NKJV

God's blessing of redemption is a gift beyond measure, a cause for thanksgiving! Make thanksgiving a habit, a regular part of your daily routine. When you slow down and express your gratitude to the One who made you, you enrich your life and the lives of those around you. Dietrich Bonhoeffer observed, "It is only with gratitude that life becomes rich."

God sent His only Son to die, rise, and conquer death for you. God has given you the priceless gifts of eternal love and eternal life. These great gifts stir reverence and gratitude in our hearts.

Embrace and respond to this gratefulness. Let it show on your face, in your words, and in your outlook. The effects of gratitude will be visible to you and those around you. Live in the joy of thanksgiving to the Lord!

> Thanksgiving is good but Thanksliving is better.
>
> —
>
> *Jim Gallery*

MORE PROMISES FROM GOD'S WORD

Thanks be to God for His indescribable gift.

2 Corinthians 9:15 HCSB

And let the peace of the Messiah, to which you were also called in one body, control your hearts. Be thankful.

Colossians 3:15 HCSB

Therefore as you have received Christ Jesus the Lord, walk in Him, rooted and built up in Him and established in the faith, just as you were taught, and overflowing with thankfulness.

Colossians 2:6-7 HCSB

It is good to give thanks to the Lord, and to sing praises to Your name, O Most High.

Psalm 92:1 NKJV

In everything give thanks; for this is the will of God in Christ Jesus for you.

1 Thessalonians 5:18 NKJV

MORE GREAT IDEAS

The words "thank" and "think" come from the same root word. If we would think more, we would thank more.

Warren Wiersbe

Though I know intellectually how vulnerable I am to pride and power, I am the last one to know when I succumb to their seduction. That's why spiritual Lone Rangers are so dangerous—and why we must depend on trusted brothers and sisters who love us enough to tell us the truth.

Chuck Colson

The act of thanksgiving is a demonstration of the fact that you are going to trust and believe God.

Kay Arthur

God has promised that if we harvest well with the tools of thanksgiving, there will be seeds for planting in the spring.

Gloria Gaither

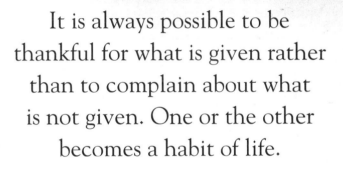

It is always possible to be
thankful for what is given rather
than to complain about what
is not given. One or the other
becomes a habit of life.

—

Elisabeth Elliot

A TIMELY TIP

Make your thanksgiving known to God. Tell Him often throughout the day and notice the difference in your outlook.

A PRAYER FOR TODAY

Lord, let me be thankful. Your blessings are priceless and eternal. I praise You, Lord, for Your gifts and, most of all, for Your Son. Amen

YOUR OWN THOUGHTS ABOUT
THANKING GOD FOR HIS BLESSINGS

CHAPTER 25

REDEEMED AND HUMBLED

*Clothe yourselves with humility
toward one another,
because God resists the proud,
but gives grace to the humble.*

—

1 Peter 5:5 HCSB

We have heard the phrases on countless occasions: "He's a self-made man" or "She's a self-made woman." In truth, none of us are self-made. We all owe countless debts that we can never repay, starting with our Father in heaven and continuing with parents, teachers, friends, spouses, family members, coworkers, fellow believers . . . and the list goes on.

We who have been redeemed have a profound reason to be humble: We have been refashioned by Jesus Christ, and that salvation came not because of our own good works but because of God's grace. We are "God-made" and "Christ-saved." How, then, can we be boastful? With humility and gratefulness, we should gladly give Him all the glory.

> Let another praise you, and not your own mouth—a stranger, and not your own lips.
>
> —
>
> *Proverbs 27:2 HCSB*

MORE PROMISES FROM GOD'S WORD

But He said to me, "My grace is sufficient for you, for power is perfected in weakness." Therefore, I will most gladly boast all the more about my weaknesses, so that Christ's power may reside in me.

2 Corinthians 12:9 HCSB

You will save the humble people; but Your eyes are on the haughty, that You may bring them down.

2 Samuel 22:28 NKJV

If My people who are called by My name will humble themselves, and pray and seek My face, and turn from their wicked ways, then I will hear from heaven, and will forgive their sin and heal their land.

2 Chronicles 7:14 NKJV

Do nothing out of rivalry or conceit, but in humility consider others as more important than yourselves.

Philippians 2:3 HCSB

Jesus had a humble heart.
If He abides in us,
pride will never
dominate our lives.

—

Billy Graham

MORE GREAT IDEAS

I can usually sense that a leading is from the Holy Spirit when it calls me to humble myself, to serve somebody, to encourage somebody, or to give something away. Very rarely will the evil one lead us to do those kind of things.

Bill Hybels

Because Christ Jesus came to the world clothed in humility, he will always be found among those who are clothed with humility. He will be found among the humble people.

A. W. Tozer

All kindness and good deeds, we must keep silent. The result will be an inner reservoir of personality power.

Catherine Marshall

We are never stronger than the moment we admit we are weak.

Beth Moore

> Humility is an attitude.
> The Lord is high and lifted up, and we are
> supposed to take a position of lowliness.
>
> —
>
> *Franklin Graham*

A PRAYER FOR TODAY

Lord, You are great, and I am human. Keep me humble, and keep me mindful that all my gifts come from You. Amen

YOUR OWN THOUGHTS ABOUT
BEING HUMBLE

CHAPTER 26

REDEEMED AND RENEWED

*But those who wait on the Lord
shall renew their strength; they shall
mount up with wings like eagles,
they shall run and not be weary,
they shall walk and not faint.*

—

Isaiah 40:31 NKJV

Today is literally brimming with possibilities. One of the first that leads to many more is the shedding of the old life and old habits that harm our lives and get in the way of our relationship with God. He encourages us to ask him for help with this in His Word. The psalmist writes, "Create in me a clean heart, O God, and renew a right spirit within me" (Psalm 51:10, ESV).

Paul writes in his letter to the Romans this encouragement, "Do not be conformed to this world, but be transformed by the renewal of your mind, that by testing you may discern what is the will of God, what is good and acceptable and perfect" (Romans 12:2, ESV).

> Christ came when all things were growing old. He made them new.
>
> —
>
> *St. Augustine*

Even though we may not be conscious of it, God is always working in us and through us, renewing our spirits and refocusing our vision.

Today, embrace the work God is doing in you. Set out upon your life's journey with a renewed sense of purpose and hope. Remember that God has the power to make all things new, including you.

MORE PROMISES FROM GOD'S WORD

Finally, brothers, rejoice. Be restored, be encouraged, be of the same mind, be at peace, and the God of love and peace will be with you.

2 Corinthians 13:11 HCSB

But may the God of all grace, who called us to His eternal glory by Christ Jesus, after you have suffered a while, perfect, establish, strengthen, and settle you.

1 Peter 5:10 NKJV

Therefore if anyone is in Christ, he is a new creature; the old things passed away; behold, new things have come.

2 Corinthians 5:17 HCSB

You are being renewed in the spirit of your minds; you put on the new man, the one created according to God's likeness in righteousness and purity of the truth.

Ephesians 4:23-24 HCSB

MORE GREAT IDEAS

The amazing thing about Jesus is that He doesn't just patch up our lives, He gives us a brand new sheet, a clean slate to start over, all new.

Gloria Gaither

He is the God of wholeness and restoration.

Stormie Omartian

But while relaxation is one thing, refreshment is another. We need to drink frequently and at length from God's fresh springs, to spend time in the Scripture, time in fellowship with Him, time worshiping Him.

Ruth Bell Graham

One reason so much American Christianity is a mile wide and an inch deep is that Christians are simply tired. Sometimes you need to kick back and rest for Jesus' sake.

Dennis Swanberg

Troubles we bear trustfully
can bring us a fresh vision of God
and a new outlook on life,
an outlook of peace and hope.

—

Billy Graham

A TIMELY TIP

God came to give you peace. Rejoice as He renews your spirit!

A PRAYER FOR TODAY

Dear Lord, You make all things new. I am a new creature in Christ Jesus. When I fall short in my commitment, renew my effort and my enthusiasm. When I am weak or worried, restore my strength. Amen

YOUR OWN THOUGHTS ABOUT
GOD'S POWER TO RENEW YOUR STRENGTH

CHAPTER 27

REDEEMED AND FREE

Praise be to the God and Father of our Lord Jesus Christ! In his great mercy he has given us new birth into a living hope through the resurrection of Jesus Christ from the dead....

—

1 Peter 1:3 NIV

God's heart is overflowing with love, and His power to forgive, like His love, is infinite. Despite our shortcomings, despite our mistakes, God offers us immediate forgiveness when we ask Him. Despite our past failures, despite our weaknesses, God loves us still.

We are free! Free from death, free from bondage in sin. Because God has redeemed us from our sins—because He loves us despite our imperfections and frailties—we too should be quick to freely forgive others. As recipients of God's great mercy, we should be merciful. Living free means the ability to make choices. Let us choose in our freedom to love the Lord, each other, and live in the joy of this incredible gift.

> Jesus draws near to those who are afflicted and persecuted and criticized and ostracized.
>
> —
>
> *Anne Graham Lotz*

MORE PROMISES FROM GOD'S WORD

For the LORD your God is a merciful God. . . .

Deuteronomy 4:31 NIV

But because of his great love for us, God, who is rich in mercy, made us alive with Christ even when we were dead in transgressions—it is by grace you have been saved.

Ephesians 2:4-5 NIV

But the mercy of the LORD is from everlasting to everlasting upon them that fear him, and his righteousness unto children's children. . . .

Psalm 103:17 KJV

O praise the LORD, all ye nations: praise him, all ye people. For his merciful kindness is great toward us: and the truth of the LORD endureth for ever. Praise ye the LORD.

Psalm 117 KJV

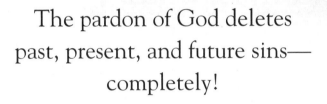

The pardon of God deletes
past, present, and future sins—
completely!

—

Franklin Graham

MORE GREAT IDEAS

Mercy is an attribute of God, an infinite and inexhaustible energy within the divine nature which disposes God to be actively compassionate.

A. W. Tozer

For God is, indeed, a wonderful Father who longs to pour out His mercy upon us, and whose majesty is so great that He can transform us from deep within.

St. Teresa of Avila

It doesn't matter how big the sin is or how small, it doesn't matter whether it was spontaneous or malicious. God will forgive you if you come to Him and confess your sin!

Anne Graham Lotz

God expects us to forgive others as He has forgiven us; we are to follow His example by having a forgiving heart.

Vonette Bright

God is always ready to meet people wherever they are, no matter how dreadful their sins may seem.

—

Jim Cymbala

A PRAYER FOR TODAY

Dear Lord, You have blessed me so much with the freedom You won for me. Enable me to use this freedom to be merciful toward others, Father, just as You have been merciful toward me. Amen

YOUR OWN THOUGHTS ABOUT FREEDOM

CHAPTER 28

REDEEMED AND NOT WHO I USED TO BE

*But grow in the grace and knowledge of
our Lord and Savior Jesus Christ.
To Him be the glory both now
and to the day of eternity.*

—

2 Peter 3:18 HCSB

The journey toward spiritual maturity lasts a lifetime. As Christians who have received redemption from God's Son, we can continue to grow in the love and the knowledge of our Savior as long as we live. If we study God's Word, if we obey His commandments, and if we live in the center of His will, we will not be "stagnant" believers; we will, instead, be growing and that's exactly what God wants for our lives.

Many of life's most important lessons are painful to learn. During times of heartbreak and hardship, God stands ready to protect us. As Psalm 147 promises, "He heals the brokenhearted and bandages their wounds" (NCV). In His own time and according to His master plan, God will heal us.

Spiritual growth need not take place only in times of adversity. We must seek to grow in our knowledge and love of the Lord every day that we live. In those quiet moments when we open our hearts to God, the One who made us keeps remaking us. He gives us direction, perspective, wisdom, and courage. The appropriate moment to accept those spiritual gifts is the present one.

MORE PROMISES FROM GOD'S WORD

I want their hearts to be encouraged and joined together in love, so that they may have all the riches of assured understanding, and have the knowledge of God's mystery—Christ.

Colossians 2:2 HCSB

For You, O God, have tested us; You have refined us as silver is refined. You brought us into the net; You laid affliction on our backs. You have caused men to ride over our heads; we went through fire and through water; but You brought us out to rich fulfillment.

Psalm 66:10–12 NKJV

Now may the God of hope fill you with all joy and peace in believing, so that you may overflow with hope by the power of the Holy Spirit.

Romans 15:13 HCSB

For this reason also, since the day we heard this, we haven't stopped praying for you. We are asking that you may be filled with the knowledge of His will in all wisdom and spiritual understanding.

Colossians 1:9 HCSB

MORE GREAT IDEAS

I'm not what I want to be. I'm not what I'm going to be. But, thank God, I'm not what I was!

Gloria Gaither

Enjoy the adventure of receiving God's guidance. Taste it, revel in it, appreciate the fact that the journey is often a lot more exciting than arriving at the destination.

Bill Hybels

When you're through changing, you're through!

John Maxwell

Recently I've been learning that life comes down to this: God is in everything. Regardless of what difficulties I am experiencing at the moment, or what things aren't as I would like them to be, I look at the circumstances and say, "Lord, what are you trying to teach me?"

Catherine Marshall

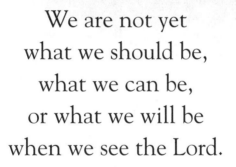

We are not yet
what we should be,
what we can be,
or what we will be
when we see the Lord.

—

John MacArthur

A TIMELY TIP

Make the seeking of spiritual growth a daily habit. Be in the Word, pray, and live in Christ.

A PRAYER FOR TODAY

Dear Lord, the Bible tells me that You are at work in my life, continuing to help me grow and to mature in my faith. Show me Your wisdom, Father, and let me live according to Your Word and Your will. Amen

YOUR OWN THOUGHTS ABOUT
WAYS TO GROW SPIRITUALLY

CHAPTER 29

REDEEMED
FOR ALL TIME

For God loved the world in this way:
He gave His only Son, so that everyone
who believes in Him will not perish
but have eternal life.

—

John 3:16 HCSB

Because you've been redeemed, your life here on earth is a step on the journey for a far different life to come: the eternal life that God promises to those who welcome Jesus into their hearts.

Our vision for the future is finite. God's vision is not burdened by such limitations: His plans extend throughout all eternity. Thus, God's plans for you are not limited to the ups and downs of everyday life. Your Heavenly Father has bigger things in mind.

How marvelous it is that God became a man and walked among us. Had He not chosen to do so, we might feel removed from a distant Creator. But ours is not a distant God. Ours is a God who understands far better than we ever could the essence of what it means to be human.

God understands our hopes, our fears, and our temptations. He understands what it means to be angry and what it costs to forgive. He knows the heart, the conscience, and the soul of every person who has ever lived, including you.

> Slowly and surely, we learn the great secret of life, which is to know God.
>
> —
>
> *Oswald Chambers*

As you struggle with the inevitable hardships and occasional disappointments of life, remember that God has invited you to accept His abundance not only for today but also for all eternity. So keep things in perspective. Although you will inevitably encounter occasional defeats in this world, you'll have all eternity to celebrate the ultimate victory.

Turn your life over
to Christ today, and your life
will never be the same.

—

Billy Graham

MORE PROMISES FROM GOD'S WORD

And this is the testimony: God has given us eternal life, and this life is in His Son. The one who has the Son has life. The one who doesn't have the Son of God does not have life.

1 John 5:11-12 HCSB

Jesus said to her, "I am the resurrection and the life. The one who believes in Me, even if he dies, will live. Everyone who lives and believes in Me will never die— ever. Do you believe this?"

John 11:25-26 HCSB

I have written these things to you who believe in the name of the Son of God, so that you may know that you have eternal life.

1 John 5:13 HCSB

In a little while the world will see Me no longer, but you will see Me. Because I live, you will live too.

John 14:19 HCSB

MORE GREAT IDEAS

And because we know Christ is alive, we have hope for the present and hope for life beyond the grave.

Billy Graham

Someday you will read in the papers that Moody is dead. Don't you believe a word of it. At that moment I shall be more alive than I am now. I was born of the flesh in 1837, I was born of the spirit in 1855. That which is born of the flesh may die. That which is born of the Spirit shall live forever.

D. L. Moody

Once a man is united to God, how could he not live forever? Once a man is separated from God, what can he do but wither and die?

C. S. Lewis

Let us see the victorious Jesus, the conqueror of the tomb, the one who defied death. And let us be reminded that we, too, will be granted the same victory.

Max Lucado

Jesus came down from heaven, revealing exactly
what God is like, offering eternal life and
a personal relationship with God,
on the condition of our rebirth—a rebirth made
possible through His own death on the cross.

—

Anne Graham Lotz

A PRAYER FOR TODAY

Lord, You have given me the gift of eternal life through Christ Jesus. I praise You for that priceless gift. Because I am saved, I will share the story of Your Son and the glory of my salvation with a world that desperately needs Your grace. Amen

YOUR OWN THOUGHTS ABOUT
THE GIFT OF ETERNAL LIFE

CHAPTER 30

REDEEMED AND FOLLOWING GOD'S SON

*"Follow Me," Jesus told them, "and
I will make you into fishers of men!"
Immediately they left their nets
and followed Him.*

—

Mark 1:17-18 HCSB

Jesus walks with you. Are you walking with Him? Has He made a radical difference in your life—an unmistakable difference in the way you think and the way you behave? Hopefully, you can answer the questions with a resounding yes. After all, Jesus loved you so much that He endured unspeakable humiliation and suffering and conquered death with His resurrection. And He did it for you.

> A believer comes to Christ; a disciple follows after Him.
>
> —
>
> *Vance Havner*

You've been redeemed by God's Son. So, how will you respond to Him? Will you take up His cross and follow Him, or will you choose another path? When you place your hopes squarely at the foot of the cross, when you place Jesus squarely at the center of your life, you will become a real follower, and that's precisely the kind of disciple Christ wants you to be.

The old familiar hymn begins, "What a friend we have in Jesus . . . ." No truer words were ever penned. Jesus is the sovereign Friend and ultimate Savior of mankind. Today provides yet another glorious opportunity to place yourself in the service of the One from Galilee. May you seek His will, may you trust His word, and may you walk in His footsteps. When you do, you'll demonstrate that your acquaintance with the Master is not a passing fancy, but is, instead, the cornerstone and the touchstone of your life.

When we truly walk with God throughout our day, life slowly starts to fall into place.

—

Bill Hybels

MORE PROMISES FROM GOD'S WORD

But whoever keeps His word, truly in him the love of God is perfected. This is how we know we are in Him: the one who says he remains in Him should walk just as He walked.

1 John 2:5-6 HCSB

The one who loves his life will lose it, and the one who hates his life in this world will keep it for eternal life. If anyone serves Me, he must follow Me. Where I am, there My servant also will be. If anyone serves Me, the Father will honor him.

John 12:25-26 HCSB

You did not choose Me, but I chose you. I appointed you that you should go out and produce fruit, and that your fruit should remain, so that whatever you ask the Father in My name, He will give you.

John 15:16 HCSB

Then He said to them all, "If anyone wants to come with Me, he must deny himself, take up his cross daily, and follow Me."

Luke 9:23 HCSB

Being a Christian is more than
just an instantaneous conversion;
it is like a daily process
whereby you grow to be
more and more like Christ.

—

Billy Graham

MORE GREAT IDEAS

Imagine the spiritual strength the disciples drew from walking hundreds of miles with Jesus . . . 3 John 4.

Jim Maxwell

Our responsibility is to feed from Him, to stay close to Him, to follow Him—because sheep easily go astray—so that we eternally experience the protection and companionship of our Great Shepherd the Lord Jesus Christ.

Franklin Graham

A disciple is a follower of Christ. That means you take on His priorities as your own. His agenda becomes your agenda. His mission becomes your mission.

Charles Stanley

To walk out of His will is to walk into nowhere.

C. S. Lewis

Heaven is a literal and specific place
promised and prepared by Jesus
for those who follow Him.

—

Bill Bright

A PRAYER FOR TODAY

Dear Lord, You sent Jesus to redeem the world and to redeem me. Thank You, and guide me as I follow Him. Amen

YOUR OWN THOUGHTS ABOUT
FOLLOWING AND SHARING CHRIST

BIBLE VERSES TO CONSIDER

WORRY

Give all your worries and cares to God, for he cares about what happens to you.

1 Peter 5:6 NLT

The Lord himself will go before you. He will be with you; he will not leave you or forget you. Don't be afraid and don't worry.

Deuteronomy 31:8 NCV

I will be with you when you pass through the waters . . . when you walk through the fire . . . the flame will not burn you. For I the Lord your God, the Holy One of Israel, and your Savior.

Isaiah 43:2-3 HCSB

Therefore do not worry about tomorrow, for tomorrow will worry about itself. Each day has enough trouble of its own.

Matthew 6:34 NIV

Give your worries to the Lord, and he will take care of you. He will never let good people down.

Psalm 55:22 NCV

PRAYER

"Relax, Daniel," he continued, "don't be afraid. From the moment you decided to humble yourself to receive understanding, your prayer was heard, and I set out to come to you."

Daniel 10:12 MSG

If you don't know what you're doing, pray to the Father. He loves to help. You'll get his help, and won't be condescended to when you ask for it. Ask boldly, believingly, without a second thought. People who "worry their prayers" are like wind-whipped waves. Don't think you're going to get anything from the Master that way, adrift at sea, keeping all your options open.

James 1:5-8 MSG

Rejoice always, pray without ceasing, in everything give thanks; for this is the will of God in Christ Jesus for you.

1 Thessalonians 5:16-18 NKJV

I want men everywhere to lift up holy hands in prayer, without anger or disputing.

1 Timothy 2:8 NIV

WORSHIP

A time is coming and has now come when the true worshipers will worship the Father in spirit and truth, for they are the kind of worshipers the Father seeks. God is spirit, and his worshipers must worship in spirit and in truth.

John 4:23-24 NIV

For it is written, "You shall worship the Lord your God, and Him only you shall serve."

Matthew 4:10 NKJV

But seek first his kingdom and his righteousness, and all these things will be given to you as well.

Matthew 6:33 NIV

God lifted him high and honored him far beyond anyone or anything, ever, so that all created beings in heaven and earth, even those long ago dead and buried, will bow in worship before this Jesus Christ, and call out in praise that he is the Master of all.

Philippians 2:9-11 MSG

MIRACLES

Is anything impossible for the LORD?

Genesis 18:14 HCSB

I assure you: The one who believes in Me will also do the works that I do. And he will do even greater works than these, because I am going to the Father.

John 14:12 HCSB

Looking at them, Jesus said, "With men it is impossible, but not with God, because all things are possible with God."

Mark 10:27 HCSB

You are the God who works wonders; You revealed Your strength among the peoples.

Psalm 77:14 HCSB

God verified the message by signs and wonders and various miracles and by giving gifts of the Holy Spirit whenever he chose to do so.

Hebrews 2:4 NLT

ATTITUDE

For the word of God is living and active. Sharper than any double-edged sword, it penetrates even to dividing soul and spirit, joints and marrow; it judges the thoughts and attitudes of the heart.

Hebrews 4:12 NIV

Therefore, since Christ suffered in his body, arm yourselves also with the same attitude, because he who has suffered in his body is done with sin. As a result, he does not live the rest of his earthly life for evil human desires, but rather for the will of God.

1 Peter 4:1-2 NIV

Your attitude should be the same as that of Christ Jesus: Who, being in very nature God, did not consider equality with God something to be grasped, but made himself nothing, taking the very nature of a servant, being made in human likeness. And being found in appearance as a man, he humbled himself and became obedient to death—even death on a cross!

Philippians 2:5-8 NIV

DIFFICULT DAYS

We take the good days from God—why not also the bad days?

Job 2:10 MSG

We are hard pressed on every side, yet not crushed; we are perplexed, but not in despair.

2 Corinthians 4:8 NKJV

Now I take limitations in stride, and with good cheer, these limitations that cut me down to size—abuse, accidents, opposition, bad breaks. I just let Christ take over! And so the weaker I get, the stronger I become.

2 Corinthians 12:10 MSG

Consider it pure joy, my brothers, whenever you face trials of many kinds, because you know that the testing of your faith develops perseverance.

James 1:2-3 NIV

Whatever has been born of God conquers the world. This is the victory that has conquered the world: our faith.

1 John 5:4 HCSB

ANGER

And the servant of the Lord must not strive; but be gentle unto all men, apt to teach, patient; in meekness instructing those that oppose themselves . . . .

2 Timothy 2:24-25 KJV

Let all bitterness, and wrath, and anger, and clamor, and evil speaking, be put away from you, with all malice: and be ye kind one to another, tender-hearted, forgiving one another, even as God for Christ's sake hath forgiven you.

Ephesians 4:31-32 KJV

But I tell you that men will have to give account on the day of judgment for every careless word they have spoken. For by your words you will be acquitted, and by your words you will be condemned.

Matthew 12:36-37 NIV

But I tell you that anyone who is angry with his brother is subject to judgment.

Matthew 5:22 NIV

INTEGRITY

Till I die, I will not deny my integrity. I will maintain my righteousness and never let go of it; my conscience will not reproach me as long as I live.

Job 27:5-6 NIV

People with integrity have firm footing, but those who follow crooked paths will slip and fall.

Proverbs 10:9 NLT

The integrity of the upright will guide them.

Proverbs 11:3 NKJV

Love and truth form a good leader; sound leadership is founded on loving integrity.

Proverbs 20:28 MSG

Not only so, but we also rejoice in our sufferings, because we know that suffering produces perseverance; perseverance, character; and character, hope.

Romans 5:3-4 NIV

ACCEPTANCE

Shall I not drink from the cup the Father has given me?

John 18:11 NLT

He is the Lord. Let him do what he thinks is best.

1 Samuel 3:18 NCV

The Lord says, "Forget what happened before, and do not think about the past. Look at the new thing I am going to do. It is already happening. Don't you see it? I will make a road in the desert and rivers in the dry land."

Isaiah 43:18-19 NCV

He said, "I came naked from my mother's womb, and I will be stripped of everything when I die. The LORD gave me everything I had, and the LORD has taken it away. Praise the name of the LORD!"

Job 1:21 NLT

Give in to God, come to terms with him and everything will turn out just fine.

Job 22:21 MSG

GRATITUDE

Everything created by God is good, and nothing is to be rejected, if it is received with gratitude; for it is sanctified by means of the word of God and prayer.

1 Timothy 4:4-5 NASB

As you therefore have received Christ Jesus the Lord, so walk in Him, having been firmly rooted and now being built up in Him and established in your faith, just as you were instructed, and overflowing with gratitude.

Colossians 2:6-7 NASB

Let the message about the Messiah dwell richly among you, teaching and admonishing one another in all wisdom, and singing psalms, hymns, and spiritual songs, with gratitude in your hearts to God.

Colossians 3:16 HCSB

Therefore, since we receive a kingdom which cannot be shaken, let us show gratitude, by which we may offer to God an acceptable service with reverence and awe . . . .

Hebrews 12:28 NASB

LAUGHTER

There is a time for everything, and a season for every activity under heaven . . . a time to weep and a time to laugh, a time to mourn and a time to dance . . . .

Ecclesiastes 3:1, 4 NIV

Shout for joy to the LORD, all the earth, burst into jubilant song with music; make music to the LORD with the harp, with the harp and the sound of singing, with trumpets and the blast of the ram's horn—shout for joy before the LORD, the King.

Psalm 98:4-6 NIV

Nehemiah said, "Go and enjoy choice food and sweet drinks, and send some to those who have nothing prepared. This day is sacred to our Lord. Do not grieve, for the joy of the LORD is your strength."

Nehemiah 8:10 NIV

A cheerful heart is good medicine.

Proverbs 17:22 NIV

HOPE

The lines of purpose in your lives never grow slack, tightly tied as they are to your future in heaven, kept taut by hope.

Colossians 1:5 MSG

Let us hold fast the confession of our hope without wavering, for He who promised is faithful.

Hebrews 10:23 NASB

Now faith is the substance of things hoped for, the evidence of things not seen.

Hebrews 11:1 KJV

I can do everything through him that gives me strength.

Philippians 4:13 NIV

This hope we have as an anchor of the soul, a hope both sure and steadfast.

Hebrews 6:19 NASB

GOD'S LOVE

We know how much God loves us, and we have put our trust in him. God is love, and all who live in love live in God, and God lives in them.

1 John 4:16 NLT

As the Father loved Me, I also have loved you; abide in My love.

John 15:9 NKJV

For God so loved the world, that he gave his only begotten Son, that whosoever believeth in him should not perish, but have everlasting life.

John 3:16 KJV

The unfailing love of the LORD never ends! By his mercies we have been kept from complete destruction.

Lamentations 3:22 NLT

His banner over me was love.

Song of Solomon 2:4 KJV

ENCOURAGEMENT

So encourage each other and give each other strength, just as you are doing now.

1 Thessalonians 5:11 NCV

Encourage each other. Live in harmony and peace. Then the God of love and peace will be with you.

2 Corinthians 13:11 NLT

So don't lose a minute in building on what you've been given, complementing your basic faith with good character, spiritual understanding, alert discipline, passionate patience, reverent wonder, warm friendliness, and generous love, each dimension fitting into and developing the others.

2 Peter 1:5-7 MSG

Watch the way you talk. Let nothing foul or dirty come out of your mouth. Say only what helps, each word a gift.

Ephesians 4:29 MSG

ABOUT
BIG DADDY Weave

Big Daddy Weave formed when its members were students at the University of Mobile. They stepped into the spotlight in 2002 with the release of their second album *One and Only*, which debuted in SoundScan's Christian Top 5 and saw the group nominated as Dove Awards New Artist of the Year. Their 2010 album *Christ Is Come* won a Dove Award for Christmas Album of the Year, and they recently released their first greatest hits compilation, *The Ultimate Collection*. They have been honored at ASCAP's Christian Music Awards, were chosen for the WOW Hits compilations in five of the last six years, and are one of the 10 most played artists on Christian radio over the past decade. Their song "Redeemed" spent 12 weeks at the top of the Christian radio charts and has impacted hundreds of thousands with the message of God's redemption.